THE USBORNE
INTERNET-LINKED
LIBRARY OF SCIENCE
MIXTURES
COMPOUNDS

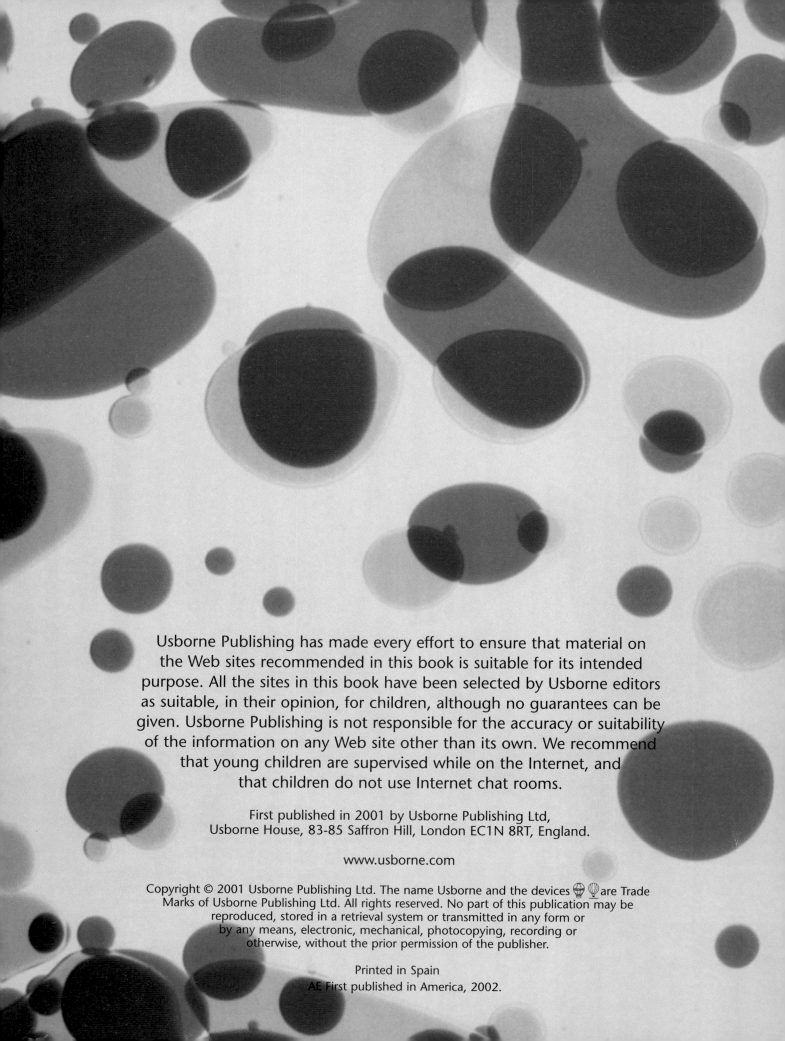

First published in 2001 by Usborne Publishing Ltd,
Usborne House, 83-85 Saffron Hill, London EC1N 8RT, England.

www.usborne.com

Printed in Spain
AE First published in America, 2002.

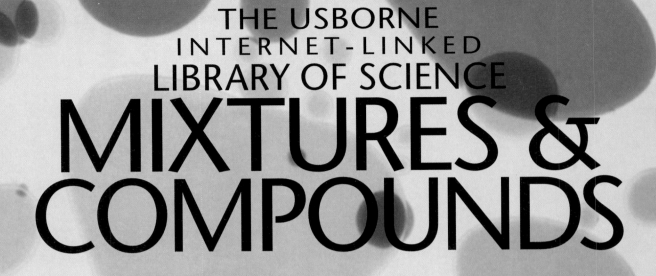

THE USBORNE
INTERNET-LINKED
LIBRARY OF SCIENCE
MIXTURES & COMPOUNDS

Alastair Smith, Phillip Clarke
and Corinne Henderson

Designed by Ruth Russell, Chloë Rafferty,
Karen Tomlins and Adam Constantine

Digital illustrations by Verinder Bhachu
Digital imagery by Joanne Kirkby

Edited by Laura Howell

Cover design: Mary Cartwright

Consultants: Elaine Wilson and Mark Beard

Web site adviser: Lisa Watts
Editorial assistant: Valerie Modd

Managing designer: Ruth Russell
Managing editor: Judy Tatchell

INTERNET LINKS

Throughout this book, we have suggested Web sites where you can find out more about mixtures and compounds. Here are some of the things you can do on the Web sites:

- create giant bubbles, or grow your own crystals
- see how substances such as plastics are created and made into useful objects
- discover different types of reactions, and how they are used in the modern world
- take an interactive tour of the ozone hole

USBORNE QUICKLINKS

To visit the sites in this book, go to the Usborne Quicklinks Web site, where you'll find links to take you to all the sites. Just go to **www.usborne-quicklinks.com** and enter the keywords "science mixtures".

The links in Usborne Quicklinks are regularly reviewed and updated, but occasionally you may get a message that a site is unavailable. This might be temporary, so try again later, or even the next day. If any of the sites close down, we will, if possible, replace them with suitable alternatives, so you will always find an up-to-date list of sites in Usborne Quicklinks.

WHAT YOU NEED

Some Web sites need additional free programs, called plug-ins, to play sounds, or to show videos, animations or 3-D images. A message will appear on your screen if a site needs a particular plug-in. There is usually a button on the site that you can click on to download it. Alternatively, go to **www.usborne-quicklinks.com** and click on "Net Help". There you can find links to download plug-ins.

www.usborne-quicklinks.com

Go to Usborne Quicklinks and enter the keywords "science mixtures" for:

- direct links to all the Web sites in this book
- free downloadable pictures, which appear throughout this book marked with a ★ symbol

INTERNET SAFETY

When using the Internet, please make sure you follow these guidelines:

- Ask your parent's or guardian's permission before you connect to the Internet.
- If a Web site asks you to enter your name, address, e-mail address, telephone number or any other personal details, ask permission from an adult before you type anything.
- If you receive an e-mail from someone you don't know, tell an adult and do not reply to the e-mail.
- Never arrange to meet with anyone you have talked to on the Internet.

NOTES FOR PARENTS

The Web sites described in this book are regularly reviewed and the links in Usborne Quicklinks are updated. However, the content of a Web site may change at any time and Usborne Publishing is not responsible for the content on any Web site other than its own. We recommend that children are supervised while on the Internet, that they do not use Internet Chat Rooms, and that you use Internet filtering software to block unsuitable material. Please ensure that your children read and follow the safety guidelines printed above. For more information, see the "Net Help" area on the Usborne Quicklinks Web site.

DOWNLOADABLE PICTURES

Pictures in this book marked with a ★ symbol may be downloaded from Usborne Quicklinks for your own personal use, for example, to illustrate a homework report or project. The pictures are the copyright of Usborne Publishing and may not be used for any commercial or profit-related purpose.

SEE FOR YOURSELF

The *See for yourself* boxes in this book contain experiments, activities or observations which we have tested. Some recommended Web sites also contain experiments, but we have not tested all of these. This book will be used by readers of different ages and abilities, so it is important that you do not tackle an experiment on your own, either from the book or the Web, that involves equipment that you do not normally use, such as a kitchen knife or cooker. Instead, ask an adult to help you.

CONTENTS

6 Mixtures and compounds

8 Mixtures

10 Separating mixtures

12 The air

16 Compounds

18 Bonding

22 Water

26 Chemical reactions

30 Oxidation and reduction

32 Electrolysis

34 Acids and bases

38 Salts

40 Crystals

42 Organic chemistry

46 Alkanes and alkenes

48 Crude oil

50 Polymers and plastics

52 Using plastics

54 Structure of an atom

55 Facts and lists

57 Test yourself

58 A-Z of scientific terms

61 Index

64 Acknowledgements

MIXTURES AND COMPOUNDS

Most substances are either mixtures or compounds. The different substances in a mixture can easily be separated. Compounds are made up of more than one substance bonded together chemically to make an entirely new substance. A compound has different properties to its ingredients. In this book, you can investigate the many mixtures and compounds around us, including their uses and methods of separating them.

This paint is a mixture of oil and colored pigments. You can mix paints together to make different colors, but the chemical structure of the paint remains the same. A compound, on the other hand, has different properties to its original ingredients.

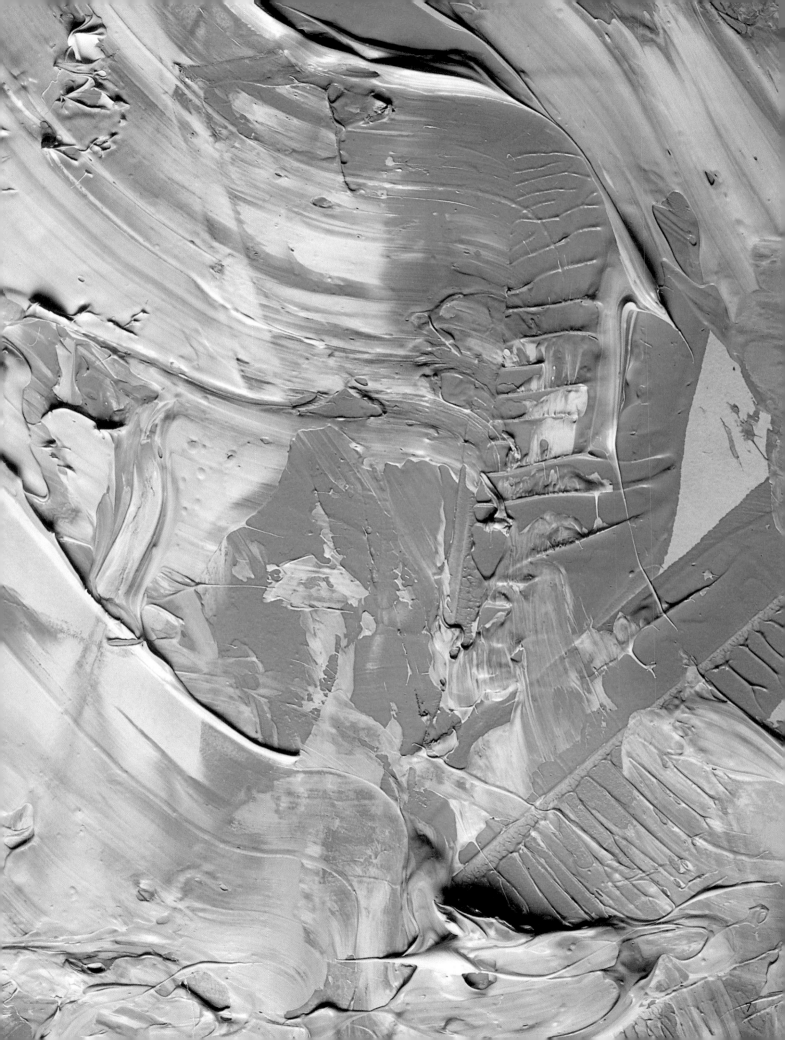

MIXTURES

Most of the natural substances around us, such as sea water and the air, are mixtures. A **mixture** is a combination of different substances that can be separated because they have different physical properties – such as different boiling points.

Ice cream is a mixture of ice, milk fat, flavorings and air.

WHAT IS A MIXTURE?

The ingredients in a mixture are not chemically bonded*, so they can usually be separated easily. For example, iron can be removed from a mixture of iron filings and sulfur using a magnet. Other methods of separating mixtures are shown on pages 10-11.

This magnet is covered with iron filings. When held in a mixture of sulfur and iron filings, the filings cling to the magnet, leaving sulfur behind.

A mixture may contain any proportion of the substances of which it is made.

The substances keep their own properties, and the mixture has all the properties of the substances, except, for example, in a solution. In this case, the boiling and freezing points may change depending on the mixture.

WHAT'S IN A MIXTURE?

Some mixtures contain two or more elements (substances made up of only one type of atom), as shown in the diagram below.

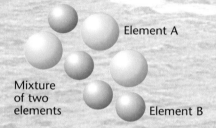

Element A

Mixture of two elements

Element B

Some mixtures contain two or more different compounds (substances made up of different atoms bonded together).

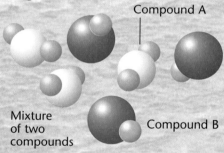

Compound A

Mixture of two compounds

Compound B

Other mixtures contain elements and compounds. Air is a mixture of elements such as oxygen, and compounds such as carbon dioxide and soot.

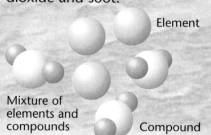

Element

Mixture of elements and compounds

Compound

TYPES OF MIXTURES

A mixture can be any combination of solids, liquids and gases. For example, air is a mixture of gases, and sea water is a mixture of salt (a solid) and water (a liquid).

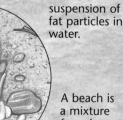

These metal tacks are made of brass, a mixture of copper and zinc. Mixtures of metals are called **alloys**.

A mixture of a solid dissolved in a liquid, such as salt in water, is called a **solution**. The liquid is called the **solvent** and the solid is called the **solute**. A solid that dissolves easily is said to be **soluble**, while a solid that won't dissolve is **insoluble**.

A mixture of solid particles floating in a liquid or a gas is called a **suspension**. Blood, milk and smoke are suspensions.

Milk is a suspension of fat particles in water.

A beach is a mixture of sand, seashells and pebbles.

MIXING LIQUIDS

Liquids that mix easily, such as ink and water, are called **miscible** liquids. Liquids that don't mix easily, such as oil and water, are said to be **immiscible**.

They can be made to mix by adding an emulsifier. An **emulsifier** makes one liquid, such as oil, break up into minute droplets in another, such as water. The resulting liquid is called an **emulsion**.

Sea water is mainly a solution of salt (sodium chloride) and water.

Blobs of oil in water. If an emulsifier is added to this mixture, the oil breaks down into tiny beads, forming an emulsion with the water.

Emulsion paint is made from water, droplets of oil, colored pigment and chemical emulsifiers.

Carbonated drinks are a mixture of two liquids (water and flavoring) and a gas (carbon dioxide). The gas makes the fizzy bubbles.

Mayonnaise is an emulsion of oil and vinegar. The emulsifier is egg yolk.

See for yourself

You can compare a solution with a mixture that contains non-soluble substances. Stir some sand into a jar of water. Then stir a spoonful of salt into a different jar of water.

The sand won't dissolve, no matter how hard you stir it. You are left with a simple mixture of water and sand.

As you stir the salt into the water, it dissolves and forms a solution. It breaks down into tiny parts and can't be seen. Both jars, though, contain mixtures.

Salt

Sand

Water

Salt dissolves in water

Internet links

Go to **www.usborne-quicklinks.com** for links to the following Web sites:

Web site 1 Learn more about solutions by making your own rock candy.

Web site 2 Find out how to make marbled paper, using the principle that oil and water do not mix.

Web site 3 Make a glitter toy using the immiscible properties of two liquids.

Web site 4 Try a simple experiment to find out how heat affects the speed at which a solid dissolves in a liquid.

SEPARATING MIXTURES

There are a number of different ways to separate the substances in a mixture. The method that you choose depends on the physical properties of the substances that the mixture contains.

In this coffee pot, the wire mesh separates the ground coffee from the hot drink.

DECANTATION

Decantation is a simple method of separating solid, insoluble particles from a liquid by leaving the particles to settle and pouring off the liquid.

Sand, soil and other matter settle in layers in a jar of muddy water.

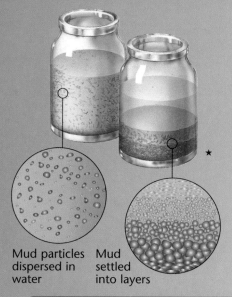

Mud particles dispersed in water

Mud settled into layers

FILTRATION

Filtration is another method of separating insoluble, solid particles from a liquid. The mixture is poured through a filter which traps the particles and only allows the molecules of liquid to pass through. This method is used in waterworks* as part of the process of producing clean drinking water.

The liquid that passes through the filter is called the **filtrate.** The solid that remains behind is the **residue**.

Filter paper traps the residue.

Filtrate

★

CHROMATOGRAPHY

Chromatography is used to analyze the substances in a mixture. The mixture is dissolved and some of the solution is put on a piece of filter paper. The substances in the solution which dissolve most easily travel farthest, and form bands of color called a **chromatogram**.

Scientists can identify the substances in a solution by comparing their chromatograms with those of known substances. This method can be used, for example, to identify the colorings used in foods.

This chemist is studying paper chromatograms to identify the chemicals used in various clothes dyes.

See for yourself

You can use chromatography (see above right) to separate the different colored chemicals that make up inks. You need a piece of filter paper or paper towel, a bowl of water and some felt-tip pens.

1. Put some spots of ink about 1in from the bottom of the paper.

2. Hang the paper over a bowl of water so that the water touches the paper but not the ink spots.

3. The paper absorbs the water. As the water reaches the blobs of ink, the dyes in the inks dissolve and are carried upwards. The dyes that dissolve most easily travel farthest.

EVAPORATION

Evaporation is a method of separating a soluble solid from the solvent* in which it is dissolved. The solution is heated until all the liquid turns to vapor (evaporates), leaving the solid behind.

Lemon juice, which is a solution of citric acid in water, separates by evaporation.

Water evaporates from boiling lemon juice. Eventually, only solid crystals of citric acid are left behind.

DISTILLATION

Distillation is a way of obtaining pure solvent, such as water, from a solution. First, the liquid is boiled. As it boils, the water evaporates into steam. This is cooled and condenses into pure water. The pure water is collected in another vessel. The other part of the solution is left behind.

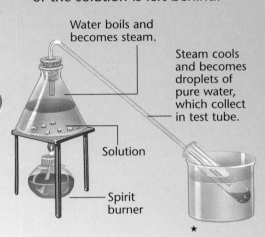

Water boils and becomes steam.

Steam cools and becomes droplets of pure water, which collect in test tube.

Solution

Spirit burner

★

CENTRIFUGING

Centrifuging separates solid particles from a suspension*. The liquid is spun around very quickly in a machine called a **centrifuge**.

This forces the solid particles to the sides of the container and the liquid can be poured or filtered off.

This is a centrifuge being used in a hospital to separate the components of human blood.

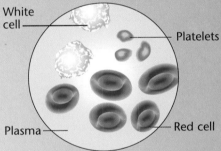

White cell

Platelets

Plasma

Red cell

Blood can be separated in a centrifuge because it is a suspension of cells and platelets in a clear fluid called plasma.

Internet links

Go to **www.usborne-quicklinks.com** for links to the following Web sites:

Web site 1 Read a detailed description of the distillation process, with some helpful diagrams.

Web site 2 Find out more about distillation and how it is used in the petroleum industry.

Web site 3 Learn about the different methods used to purify the tap water you drink.

Web site 4 An article about different types of chromatography, with details of their uses.

* Solvent, Suspension, 8.

11

THE AIR

The **air** is a mixture of gases that form a protective layer called the **atmosphere** around the Earth. Air is essential for life on Earth – for animals to breathe and for plants to make their food – and it also helps to protect the Earth from the Sun's dangerous ultraviolet rays*. The main gases in air are nitrogen and oxygen. There are also traces of the noble gases and of carbon dioxide, plus solid particles such as soot and pollen.

About 21% of air is oxygen. A molecule of oxygen (O_2) consists of two oxygen atoms bonded together.

GASES IN THE AIR

The amounts of the different gases in the air vary slightly from place to place, season to season and day to night. The pie chart below shows the average volumes of the gases as percentages.

Composition of the air

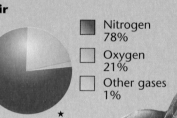

Nitrogen and oxygen are the main gases. The remaining 1% is noble gases, carbon dioxide, water vapor and pollutants such as nitrogen dioxide.

- Nitrogen 78%
- Oxygen 21%
- Other gases 1%

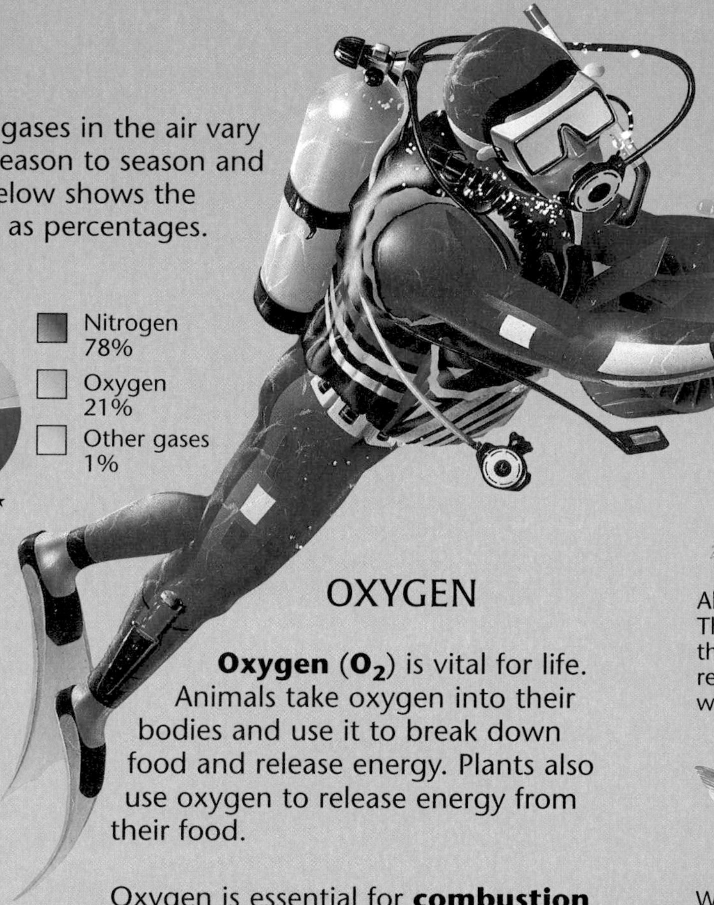

★

This diver is carrying a cylinder of compressed air on his back, which contains oxygen, to breathe underwater.

SEPARATING GASES

The gases in air can be separated by a process called **fractional distillation**. The air is cooled and compressed until the gases become liquids. This mixture is heated. Each liquid boils at a different temperature and is collected separately as it boils.

Oxygen, nitrogen and carbon dioxide are continually removed and returned to the air by living things as part of natural cycles.

OXYGEN

Oxygen (O_2) is vital for life. Animals take oxygen into their bodies and use it to break down food and release energy. Plants also use oxygen to release energy from their food.

Oxygen is essential for **combustion** (burning). If there is lots of oxygen, things will burn very quickly. If there is no oxygen, nothing can burn.

All animals need oxygen. They take in oxygen when they breathe in, and release carbon dioxide when they breathe out.

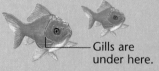

Gills are under here.

When water is gulped in by a fish, it passes over its gills. The gills take oxygen that is dissolved in the water so that it can be used in the body.

CARBON DIOXIDE

Carbon dioxide (CO_2) is a compound made of the elements carbon and oxygen. The air contains about 0.03% carbon dioxide.

A carbon dioxide (CO_2) molecule has a carbon atom and two oxygen atoms.

Carbon dioxide is slightly soluble in water, dissolving to form a weak solution of carbonic acid. Carbon dioxide is part of the carbon cycle*. Animals breathe it out. Plants release it, and use it in photosynthesis*.

Most substances cannot burn in carbon dioxide. That is why it is used in fire extinguishers.

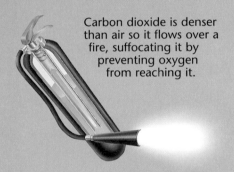

Carbon dioxide is denser than air so it flows over a fire, suffocating it by preventing oxygen from reaching it.

Fuels containing carbon, such as wood, coal and gasoline, produce carbon dioxide when they burn. Because we now burn so much fuel, the amount of carbon dioxide in the air is increasing. This has led to problems of global warming (see *Greenhouse Effect*, page 15).

See for yourself

Try this test to see how carbon dioxide gas puts out fire.

Light a small candle. Put five tablespoons of vinegar into a bottle. Add half a tablespoon of baking soda. As the mixture fizzes, hold the mouth of the bottle near the candle, making sure none of the liquid escapes.

Small candle

The candle goes out as carbon dioxide from the reaction prevents oxygen from reaching the flame.

AIR QUALITY

Many polluting substances are released into the air from industrial chimneys. Inside many chimneys are filters and neutralizing substances which make waste gases safer. Samples of the gases released are frequently taken and levels of pollution checked.

The cooling tower below releases harmless water vapor into the air. Waste gases from the tall chimney on the right need to be filtered or neutralized before they are released, to reduce pollution.

THE NOBLE GASES

The six **noble gases** found in the air are the only elements that exist as single atoms. They are all very unreactive and they rarely form molecules.

Argon (Ar) is often used to fill the space inside household light bulbs. It is so unreactive that the glowing filament does not react with it and burn out. **Krypton (Kr)** is used inside fluorescent tubes. **Neon (Ne)** glows orange-red when electricity passes through it, so it is used in neon lights and, with sodium, in street lamps.

Xenon (Xe) is used in flash photography. **Radon (Rn)** is radioactive and occurs as a result of the radioactive decay of radium, a metal element. **Helium (He)** is not known to form any compounds and it is thought to be completely unreactive. It is seven times less dense than air, so it is used in airships.

A helium-filled balloon carries these scientific instruments into the upper atmosphere.

Internet links

Go to **www.usborne-quicklinks.com** for links to the following Web sites:

Web site 1 Find out about the different gases that make up the Earth's atmosphere.

Web site 2 Images and information about neon and its uses, including a gallery of neon art.

Web site 3 Find out about helium and why helium balloons float.

Web site 4 The problem of air pollution, as presented by the Sierra Club, a US environmental organization.

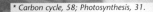

* Carbon cycle, 58; Photosynthesis, 31.

NITROGEN

Most of the air (about 78%) is **nitrogen** (**N₂**). Nitrogen is continually being recycled between the air and living things. This is called the **nitrogen cycle**.

Nitrogen molecules in the air are split up by lightning, and the freed atoms bond with oxygen to form nitrogen oxide gases. Pollution from power stations also contains these gases.

The gases react with water to become nitric acid in rainwater. This forms nitrogen salts called **nitrates** in the soil.

Fertilizers* also have a high nitrate content, so they add to the nitrates in the soil. Certain bacteria, in the roots of some plants, also add to the nitrates by taking nitrogen directly from the air and converting it into nitrates.

Plants absorb the nitrates and use them to make proteins. Animals eat plants and use the proteins in their own bodies. Ammonia and other nitrogen compounds are returned to the soil in animal waste, and when animals and plants decay after death.

The compounds are turned back into nitrates by the action of one type of bacteria in the soil. Another type takes in nitrates, breaks them down, and releases nitrogen back into the air.

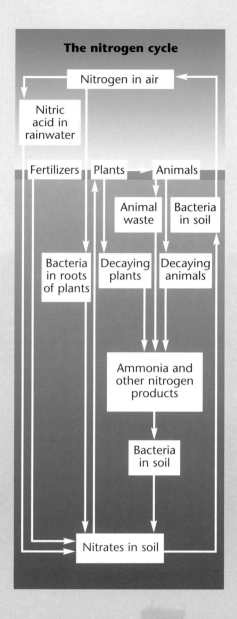

The nitrogen cycle

Nitrogen in air

Nitric acid in rainwater

Fertilizers — Plants — Animals

Animal waste — Bacteria in soil

Bacteria in roots of plants — Decaying plants — Decaying animals

Ammonia and other nitrogen products

Bacteria in soil

Nitrates in soil

USES OF NITROGEN

The main use of nitrogen is in the production of ammonia for making fertilizers*. To do this, nitrogen is combined with hydrogen. Nitrogen is also used in packaging food such as bacon and chips, because ordinary air would cause the food to oxidize* and go bad.

Liquid nitrogen is so cold and unreactive that it is used to preserve human organs for transplants.

GASES THAT POLLUTE

Carbon monoxide (**CO**) is formed when fuels burn in a limited air supply, such as in a car's engine. Most fuels burn so quickly it is difficult for them to get enough oxygen, and carbon monoxide is produced instead of carbon dioxide. Carbon monoxide is a very toxic gas that stops the red cells in animals' blood from carrying oxygen.

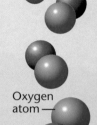

Carbon — atom

Oxygen atom —

Carbon monoxide molecules have only one atom of oxygen.

Sulfur dioxide (**SO₂**) is produced by burning fossil fuels*, especially coal. Sulfur dioxide is poisonous and causes breathing problems. It reacts with rainwater to produce acid rain (see opposite page).

Sulfur dioxide molecules

— Sulfur atom

— Oxygen atom

Particles of soot, dust and lead compounds produced by industry are other forms of pollution that can be breathed in and which settle on plants. Lead compounds are poisons that build up in the body and can cause brain damage in young children.

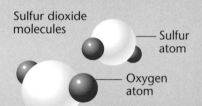

The pollution shrouding this city is made up of **smog**, a mixture of fog, smoke particles and sulfur dioxide. It can be very harmful to living things.

THE OZONE LAYER

In the upper atmosphere, oxygen atoms combine in threes, forming molecules of **ozone** (O_3). This is an allotrope* (an alternative form) of oxygen. It is a poisonous gas, but it forms a layer in the upper atmosphere that absorbs most of the Sun's harmful ultraviolet rays and protects the Earth.

Without the protective ozone layer around it, the Earth could not sustain life.

ACID RAIN

Rain is always slightly acidic from dissolved carbon dioxide, but pollutants such as sulfur dioxide and nitrogen dioxide make it more acidic. Rain containing dangerous levels of acid is called **acid rain**. It corrodes metals and damages stone buildings, and also makes the water in rivers and lakes more acidic.

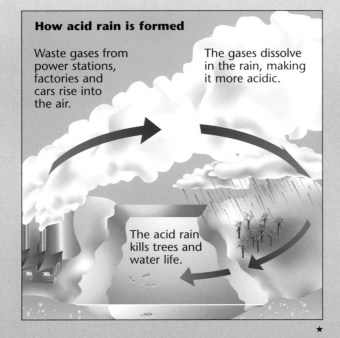

How acid rain is formed

Waste gases from power stations, factories and cars rise into the air.

The gases dissolve in the rain, making it more acidic.

The acid rain kills trees and water life.

★

Carbon dioxide in the air prevents heat from escaping from the Earth in the same way that glass prevents heat from escaping from a greenhouse.

GREENHOUSE EFFECT

This term is used to describe the way that increasing levels of carbon dioxide in the air are causing **global warming** – a rise in average temperatures around the world.

As the level of carbon dioxide increases, more heat is trapped in the Earth's atmosphere (see picture above). Even a slight rise in temperature causes the sea level to rise as the water expands, affecting winds and weather and causing some of the ice at the polar ice caps to melt. Scientists say that if the carbon dioxide level continues to increase at its present rate, average temperatures will rise by between 2°F and 8°F in the next fifty years.

Internet links

Go to **www.usborne-quicklinks.com** for links to the following Web sites:

Web site 1 Take an interactive tour of the ozone hole.

Web site 2 A long-term view of global warming.

Web site 3 Take a detailed look at the atmosphere.

Web site 4 Learn about acid rain and its effects.

Web site 5 Find information about nitrogen and the nitrogen cycle, with helpful diagrams.

See for yourself

Try this test to see how acids affect building materials.

Put a small lump of dried cement into a glass and pour in enough vinegar to cover it. Leave the experiment for two to three days.

Ethanoic acid in the vinegar reacts with the cement, which is gradually dissolved by the acid.

*Allotropes, 21.

COMPOUNDS

There are just over a hundred different chemical elements, but they combine together in many different ways to make at least two million different compound substances. A **compound** contains atoms from two or more elements chemically bonded to form a new and different substance.

Quartz is a compound of silicon and oxygen that occurs naturally in the ground. There are several types of quartz. This type is called milky quartz.

CHEMICAL FORMULAE

Every sample of a compound contains the same proportions of the elements that make it up. These can be written as a **chemical formula**, which shows the proportions of the elements in the compound.

For example, the formula for water (hydrogen oxide) is H_2O, because every two atoms of hydrogen are bonded with one atom of oxygen.

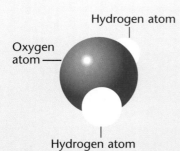

Hydrogen atom

Oxygen atom

Hydrogen atom

GROUPS OF COMPOUNDS

Compounds can be organized into separate groups, such as acids and bases, according to their chemical properties.

Compounds can also be classified according to the atoms they contain. For example, chloride compounds all contain chlorine, and oxides contain oxygen.

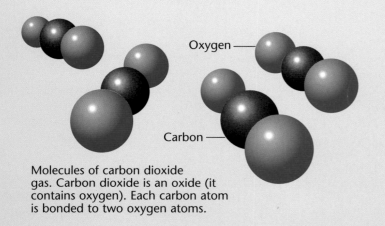

Oxygen

Carbon

Molecules of carbon dioxide gas. Carbon dioxide is an oxide (it contains oxygen). Each carbon atom is bonded to two oxygen atoms.

CHARACTERISTICS OF COMPOUNDS

Compounds have two main characteristics:
• they cannot be separated by physical means, such as filtration or evaporation, because they are chemically bonded;
• they have different properties from the elements of which they are made.

Sodium chloride (common salt), for example, is a compound made from chlorine, a poisonous gas, and sodium, a very reactive metal. When they join together, they lose their dangerous properties.

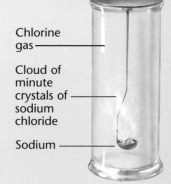

Chlorine gas

Cloud of minute crystals of sodium chloride

Sodium

When iron and sulfur are heated together, the compound formed (iron sulfide) has different properties from the original elements.

Iron and sulfur

Unlike iron, iron sulfide is not magnetic and unlike powdered sulfur, it sinks in water, as shown in the picture on the right.

After the reaction, the iron and sulfur can no longer be separated.

Water

Iron sulfide

EVERYDAY COMPOUNDS

Many of the substances around us, including things we eat, are compounds. Common salt is a compound of sodium and chlorine. Its chemical name is **sodium chloride (NaCl)**.

Glass is a compound made of calcium, silicon, oxygen and sodium.

Eggshells are made of a compound called calcium carbonate, which is also found in nature as limestone and chalk.

Butter is a mixture of compounds of carbon, hydrogen and oxygen.

Lemon juice contains citric acid, a compound of carbon, hydrogen and oxygen, mixed with water.

Eggs contain compounds of carbon, nitrogen, phosphorus, hydrogen, oxygen and sulfur.

See for yourself

Before a cake is cooked, its ingredients are a gooey mixture of different elements, compounds and other mixtures.

When the cake mixture is cooked, however, the heat causes chemical reactions* to occur, bonding the different substances into new compounds.

ORGANIC COMPOUNDS

Organic compounds all contain the element carbon. All living things are made of organic compounds. They are also used in the manufacture of plastics, detergents, paints and medicines. For more about organic compounds, see pages 42-45.

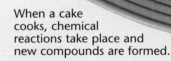

Many cosmetics contain organic compounds such as oils to give them their texture. Many of the compounds which give them color, called pigments, are inorganic.

When a cake cooks, chemical reactions take place and new compounds are formed.

Internet links

Go to **www.usborne-quicklinks.com** for links to the following Web sites:

Web site 1 See how to write chemical formulae and try a few of your own.

Web site 2 Learn about some compounds that have been of great benefit to humanity.

Web site 3 See molecular models and basic information for different compounds.

Web site 4 Play a game matching common compounds to their chemical names.

Web site 5 Information about how chemical compounds are named.

*Chemical reactions, 26-29.

BONDING

The beautiful, symmetrical shapes of ice crystals and the hard, glittery surfaces of a diamond result from the way their atoms are joined together, or **bonded**. The properties of a substance, and the way it reacts with other substances, depend on those bonds.

Crystals of ice

ELECTRON SHELLS

A **stable atom** does not need to lose or gain electrons* from the outer electron shell around its nucleus. **Unstable atoms** attempt to bond with other atoms to become stable.

Argon has a full outer shell of electrons. It is stable and is not known to bond with any other atoms.

—Electron

Most atoms have several shells of electrons. The first shell can hold up to two electrons and the second and third shells up to eight, although some atoms in compounds can have up to 18 electrons in their third shells. When a shell is full, the electrons begin a new shell.

The arrangement of electrons around the nucleus is called the **electron configuration**. This can be written as numbers after an atom's name.

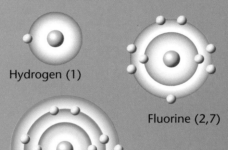

Hydrogen (1)

Fluorine (2,7)

Sodium (2,8,1)

To achieve a full or stable outer shell, an atom may share electrons with other atoms or give or take electrons from another atom (see *Covalent, Ionic* and *Metallic Bonding* on pages 19-20).

(see *Covalent, Ionic* and *Metallic Bonding* on pages 19-20).

See for yourself

The atomic number of an atom shows how many protons* it has. An atom has the same number of protons as electrons. Try calculating the electron configurations of the atoms below. Remember that they can have two electrons in the first shell, and up to eight in the second shell.

Magnesium (atomic number 12)
Argon (atomic number 18)
Nitrogen (atomic number 7)
Potassium (atomic number 19)
Silicon (atomic number 14)

(Answers on page 56.)

SHELL MODELS

Shell models, like the one on the left, are useful for understanding the make-up of an atom, but atoms don't actually look like this and the positions of electrons cannot be pinpointed with accuracy.

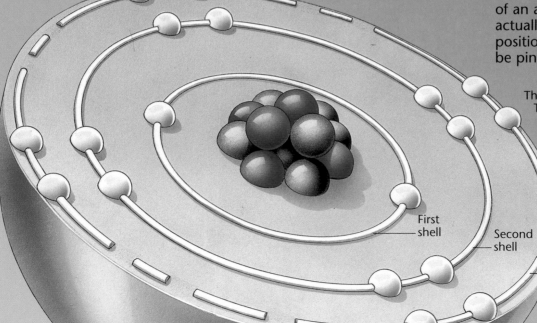

This is a shell model of an atom. There are two electrons in the first shell and eight in the second. The third shell can have up to 18 electrons.

The gaps in the third shell show where extra electrons could go if this atom were to bond with another.

First shell

Second shell

Third shell

18

*Electrons, 59; Protons, 60.

COVALENT BONDING

A **covalent bond** is formed when atoms share electrons. In most covalent elements and compounds, the atoms bond to form molecules. For example, hydrogen atoms have one electron, and a molecule of hydrogen is formed when two atoms share their electrons. This gives both atoms a full outer shell.

The atoms in carbon dioxide are also held together by covalent bonds. In this case, each of the atoms shares two electrons with its partner. This is called a **double bond**. For more about covalent bonds, see pages 42-43.

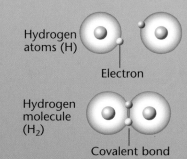

Hydrogen atoms (H)

Electron

Hydrogen molecule (H_2)

Covalent bond

Double covalent bonds

Carbon dioxide molecule (CO_2)

Oxygen atom (O)   Carbon atom (C)   Oxygen atom (O)

COVALENT SUBSTANCES

Non-metal elements, and compounds made only of non-metals, tend to form covalent bonds.

Covalent bonds between atoms in a molecule are strong, but the attraction between two molecules is not very strong. The molecules tend to break apart from each other when heated, so these substances have quite low melting and boiling points. Many are liquids or gases at room temperature.

Water, for example, is liquid at room temperature and evaporates easily. This is because the attraction between water molecules is not very strong.

Many covalent substances, such as oil, don't dissolve in water and don't conduct electricity.

Water molecules (H_2O)

The atoms in a molecule of water are held together by covalent bonds.

Oxygen atom

Hydrogen atom

Heat weakens the attraction between the water molecules in ice, and makes the ice melt.

GIANT MOLECULES

Some covalent elements, such as carbon, and many covalent compounds form giant molecules. Each atom is covalently bonded to the next atom, forming a huge, single covalent molecule that is very strong. These substances have very high melting and boiling points.

In this giant molecule of silicon dioxide, each atom of silicon (red) is bonded to three oxygen atoms behind it and one on top.

Oxygen

Silicon

Internet links

Go to **www.usborne-quicklinks.com** for links to the following Web sites:

Web site 1 Information about bonds and the different ways in which chemists represent them.

Web site 2 An in-depth look at the different types of chemical bonding, including two forms of covalent bonding.

Web site 3 Read a comprehensive article that explains bonding in all its different forms.

Web site 4 Discover the historical importance of the idea of valences.

IONIC BONDING

An atom that has gained or lost electrons becomes an **ion**. Ions have electrical charges as they do not have an equal number of positively charged protons* and negatively charged electrons.

An atom that has lost electrons becomes a **cation**. It has a positive charge. An atom that has gained electrons becomes an **anion**. An anion has a negative charge as it has more electrons than protons.

Ionic bonds are formed when the positive cations and negative anions are attracted together to form an ionic compound. Compounds made of a metal and a non-metal bond in this way. Metals are elements that form positively charged cations and non-metals are elements that form negatively charged anions. The compound is called an **ionic compound**.

This diagram shows how ions could be formed from atoms. Effectively, sodium becomes a cation with 11 protons and only 10 electrons.

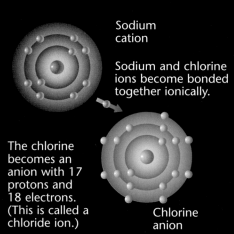

Sodium cation

Sodium and chlorine ions become bonded together ionically.

The chlorine becomes an anion with 17 protons and 18 electrons. (This is called a chloride ion.)

Chlorine anion

The type and strength of the charge is written after the ion's name. For example, Na^+ shows that sodium has lost one electron and Cl^- shows that chlorine has gained one electron. O^{2-} shows oxygen has gained two electrons.

*Protons, 60.

LATTICES

Ions with opposite charges are attracted to each other. This creates the ionic bond that holds them together. Ionic compounds are not made of separate molecules. Instead, the ions gather in a regular arrangement called an **ionic lattice**. The bonds are strong. It takes a lot of heat to break them, so ionic compounds have high melting and boiling points.

Molecular lattices are a different type of lattice. They are made of molecules that are held together by weak forces, which tend to break apart when heated. Crystals with low melting and boiling points tend to have molecules formed in this way.

METALLIC BONDING

Metallic bonding is the type of bonding found in metal elements. The atoms cling together to form a **metallic lattice** which is a regular arrangement of metal cations with free electrons traveling between them. Free electrons allow the atoms to cling together.

The forces between the electrons and the cations are strong. Most metals have high melting and boiling points, and because the electrons can move, metals can conduct heat and electricity.

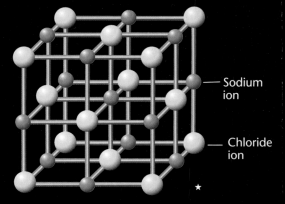

Sodium ion

Chloride ion

Ionic lattice of sodium chloride (table salt)

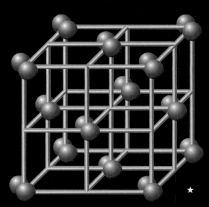

Molecular lattice of solid iodine. The molecules come apart easily.

Free-moving electrons

A giant metallic lattice of zinc

Zinc cation

VALENCY

The number of electrons an atom needs to gain or lose to form a stable outer shell of electrons is called its **valency**, or **combining power**.

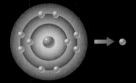

A sodium atom needs to lose one electron. Its valency is 1.

A sulfur atom needs to gain two electrons. Its valency is 2.

An atom with a stable outer shell of electrons has a valency of 0. If an atom needs to gain or lose just one electron it has a valency of 1. Valencies of 2, 3 or 4 indicate that atoms have two, three or four electrons more or less than a stable structure.

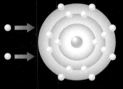

Fluorine

Fluorine has seven electrons in its outer shell. It needs to gain one electron to have a full shell so its valency is 1.

Extra electron

Phosphorus has five electrons in its outer shell and needs to gain three to form a full shell, so its valency is 3.

Phosphorus

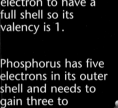

Extra electrons

The charge on an ion depends upon the valency of the atom. For instance, the oxide ion (O^{2-}) has a negative charge of 2 because oxygen has a valency of 2. Some elements can form different ions so can have more than one valency. Iron, for example, forms Fe^{2+} and Fe^{3+} ions. Roman numerals after the name, for example iron(II) and iron(III), indicate which ion is present.

ALLOTROPES

Some elements can exist in different physical forms because their atoms can bond together in different ways. The different forms are called **allotropes**. Diamond and graphite are both allotropes of the element carbon.

In **diamond**, each carbon atom is linked to four other carbon atoms and the atoms are packed tightly together. Because of this, diamond is very strong.

Diamond molecule

In **graphite**, each carbon atom bonds to just three other carbon atoms. The atoms form layers and the forces between the layers are quite weak, making graphite flaky.

Graphite molecule

Carbon has a third allotrope, called **buckminsterfullerene**, in which 60 carbon atoms are bonded together to make a hollow sphere. Many other elements, such as phosphorus, tin and sulfur, also have allotropes.

A model of a buckminsterfullerene molecule. These are usually hollow, but one in a million, like this one, traps an atom of helium during its formation.

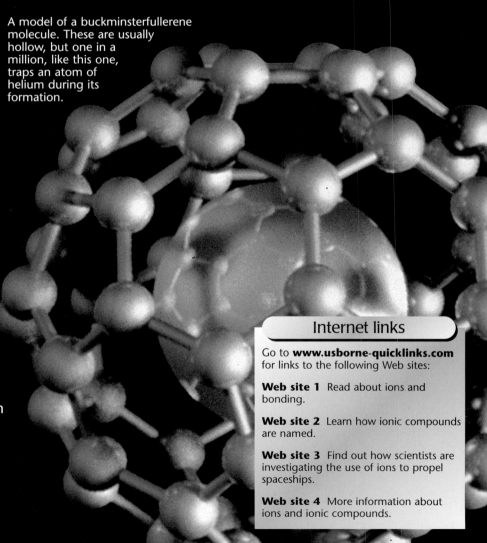

Internet links

Go to **www.usborne-quicklinks.com** for links to the following Web sites:

Web site 1 Read about ions and bonding.

Web site 2 Learn how ionic compounds are named.

Web site 3 Find out how scientists are investigating the use of ions to propel spaceships.

Web site 4 More information about ions and ionic compounds.

WATER

Water is one of the most common compounds on Earth. As well as the water in rivers and seas, all living things contain water and cannot survive without it. Blood and plant sap are mainly water. Water is a very good solvent – other substances dissolve easily in it.

About 70% of the surface of the Earth is covered with water.

WHAT IS WATER?

Water is a compound. Each molecule of water contains two atoms of hydrogen bonded to an atom of oxygen. The chemical formula for water is H_2O. The chemical name for water is **hydrogen oxide**. Water is formed when hydrogen burns in air.

Pure water, that is, water that does not contain any dissolved substances, boils at 100°C and freezes at 0°C. If water contains any dissolved substances, the boiling point is raised and the freezing point is lowered. This fact can be used to test whether a liquid is pure water.

If it is pure, the water in this beaker will boil at 100°C.

Model of a molecule of water

Oxygen atom

Hydrogen atom

Ice is the solid form of water. Icebergs float because ice is less dense than water. This huge iceberg in Antarctica rises 350ft above the sea.

When water evaporates*, it forms a gas called **water vapor**. When it freezes, it forms a solid called **ice**. Unlike most other substances, water expands when it freezes, so ice is less dense than water and it floats on water. Because of this, fish and other creatures can live in the water under the ice at the Poles.

* Evaporation, 58.

WATER AS A SOLVENT

Water is a very good **solvent**, that is, many substances dissolve easily in water to form a solution*. This is why water is rarely found in a pure state.

Many substances, like these paints, dissolve easily in water.

Water molecules have a slight electrical charge because their hydrogen atoms are grouped on one side. Because of this, ionic compounds* dissolve easily in water. Their ions* have an electrical charge and they are attracted to the charges on the water molecules.

The electrons (yellow) give this side of the molecule a slight negative charge.

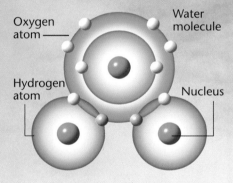

Oxygen atom

Water molecule

Hydrogen atom

Nucleus

Protons in the hydrogen nuclei give this side a slight positive charge.

A solvent, such as water, will only accept a certain amount of a substance dissolved in it. When no more will dissolve, the solution is **saturated**. The amount of solid that will dissolve usually increases if the liquid is heated.

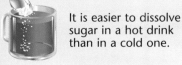

It is easier to dissolve sugar in a hot drink than in a cold one.

FIZZY DRINKS

The fizz in fizzy drinks is made by dissolving carbon dioxide gas in water, under pressure. The amount of gas that can be dissolved in a solution decreases when the pressure of the solution is decreased. When you open a carbonated drink carbon dioxide bubbles out because you are releasing (lowering) the pressure.

HARD WATER

Hard water contains dissolved minerals from rocks it has flowed over. Soap does not lather well in hard water – the minerals react with the soap to form scum. There are two types of hard water, depending on which minerals it contains.

Temporary hard water is caused by a chemical reaction between limestone and rainwater. Limestone is made of calcium carbonate, which is insoluble, and rainwater is a weak solution of carbonic acid. The acid reacts with the calcium carbonate to form calcium hydrogencarbonate which then dissolves in the water, making it hard.

Cutaway view of kettle

When temporary hard water boils in a kettle, some of the minerals are left behind and can be seen as a chalky deposit.

Chalky deposit

Permanent hard water contains calcium and magnesium compounds from rocks such as gypsum. These cannot be removed by boiling.

Water contains dissolved oxygen. This is why plants and animals can live in it.

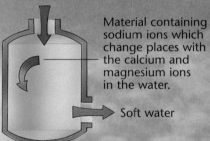

SOFTENING WATER

Minerals that make water hard can be removed by adding washing soda (water softener) or by ion exchange.

Ion exchange tank

Hard water

Material containing sodium ions which change places with the calcium and magnesium ions in the water.

Soft water

In an **ion exchange tank**, hard water containing calcium and magnesium compounds is passed through a material such as zeolite (sodium aluminum silicate). The calcium and magnesium ions are swapped for sodium ions which do not make the water hard.

Washing soda (water softener) is sodium carbonate. When added to hard water, it reacts with magnesium and calcium compounds, changing them into insoluble compounds that do not make scum.

Internet links

Go to **www.usborne-quicklinks.com** for links to the following Web sites:

Web site 1 Do a simple experiment to find out what's in a cup of water.

Web site 2 Find out why freezing water expands.

Web site 3 An advanced, but clear, explanation of the chemistry of water.

Web site 4 Lots of information about water and how it is recycled and treated.

---

* Ionic compounds, Ions, 20; Solution, 8.

THE WATER CYCLE

All the Earth's water is continually being recycled between the Earth, the atmosphere and living things. This is called the **water cycle**.

The water in rivers, lakes and seas is continually evaporating* and becoming tiny droplets of water vapor in the air. The droplets form clouds and fall again as rain, hail or snow.

CLEANING WATER

Water that has flowed over land and through rocks contains impurities. These impurities can be removed at a **waterworks**. The water is stored in reservoirs to allow solid matter to settle and then, in the waterworks, the water is filtered to remove smaller particles of mud and solids.

The water cycle

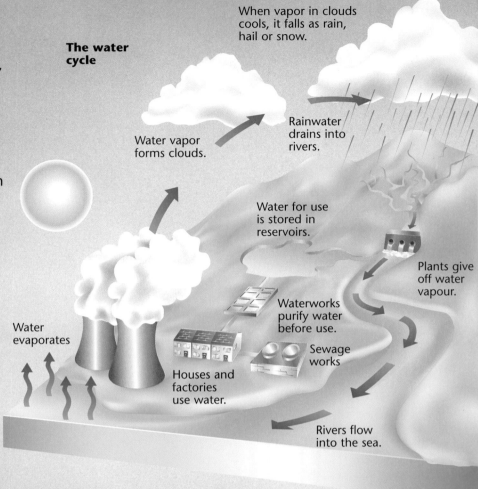

When vapor in clouds cools, it falls as rain, hail or snow.

Water vapor forms clouds.

Rainwater drains into rivers.

Water for use is stored in reservoirs.

Plants give off water vapour.

Waterworks purify water before use.

Sewage works

Water evaporates

Houses and factories use water.

Rivers flow into the sea.

A waterworks

Filter bed

Water trickles through beds of clean gravel and sand, or carbon, to remove particles of mud and other solids. After filtering, the water is treated with chlorine to kill harmful bacteria and then pumped to storage tanks and piped to houses and factories.

SEWAGE TREATMENT

Sewage (waste water) should be cleaned before it is pumped into the sea. In a **sewage works**, the water is filtered to remove waste, and then left in **sedimentation tanks** for the solid particles to settle. Bacteria decompose any remaining organic matter and break it down into harmless substances.

Here you can see part of the water cycle in action. Water vapor is rising from a rainforest and forming clouds.

* Evaporation, 59.

PURIFYING WATER

Water is a good solvent*, so it usually contains dissolved substances. Pure water can be obtained by distillation*, but a more efficient method is by **deionization**. Ions are atoms or molecules that have lost or gained an electron and so have a positive or negative electrical charge (see also page 20).

Deionization

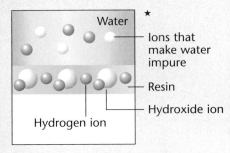

Ion exchange resin has hydrogen ions (H^+) and hydroxide ions (OH^-) clinging to it. The water contains different ions which make it impure. The water is passed through the ion exchange resin.

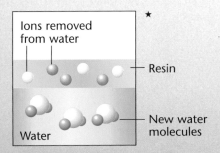

As the water goes through the resin, the ions in the water are more strongly attracted to the resin than to the water. The ions from the resin are displaced. They pass into the water, and combine to create extra molecules of water (H_2O).

WATER POLLUTION

Water pollution is caused by untreated water from houses and factories flowing into rivers and the sea.

When water contains a lot of waste, bacteria that break down organic waste matter become very numerous and use up most of the oxygen. The water becomes lifeless, except for other, harmful bacteria that can survive in water without oxygen.

Oxygen in water can also be used up by too much plant growth caused when fertilizers from farmland, and detergents that contain phosphates, drain into rivers. The oxygen in the water is used up by the plants and by bacteria that feed on the plants when they die.

POISONOUS POLLUTION

Pollution is also caused by litter, pesticides and by poisonous substances such as lead and mercury. Poisonous substances build up in the bodies of fish and may be passed on to other animals and to people. Pesticides kill tiny creatures and larger animals and disturb the balance between living things.

Untreated factory waste like this can harm the environment.

See for yourself

You can make a miniature water cycle by copying the set-up below. Leave the bowl in a sunny window, with some water in it. The heat evaporates the water, which rises and then condenses on the cool plastic, to fall into the container.

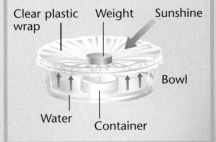

Internet links

Go to **www.usborne-quicklinks.com** for links to the following Web sites:

Web site 1 Useful information about water science.

Web site 2 Learn about water pollution – and clean up a virtual oil slick.

Web site 3 An interactive water cycle diagram with animated definitions.

Web site 4 See the water treatment process, stage by stage.

Web site 5 Find lots of information about water science and water conservation.

Distillation, 11; Solvent, 8.

CHEMICAL REACTIONS

Chemical reactions are happening around us all the time – in our digestive system when we eat, in baking a cake or in a car's engine when it's being driven. During a chemical reaction, the atoms in the substances, called the **reactants**, are rearranged to form new substances, called the **products**.

Striking a match activates the chemical reaction that takes place when the match burns.

WHAT HAPPENS IN A REACTION

During a chemical reaction, the bonds between the atoms of substances are broken. The atoms rearrange themselves and form bonds with new partners. The diagrams on the right show what happens when water and sulfur trioxide react together to form sulfuric acid.

During a chemical reaction energy is always either taken in or given out. Breaking bonds requires energy and creating new bonds releases energy. This is usually heat energy, although some reactions give off or take in light. A reaction that produces heat is called an **exothermic reaction**. If heat is taken in, it is an **endothermic reaction**. For more about these, see page 28.

Most chemical reactions also need a certain amount of energy, usually in the form of heat, to start them off. This makes the molecules in the substances move around so they collide and can react together. The minimum amount of energy needed to start off a reaction is called the **activation energy**.

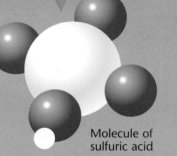

Each molecule of water (H_2O) is made of two atoms of hydrogen and one atom of oxygen. Sulfur trioxide (SO_3) is made of three atoms of oxygen bonded to one atom of sulfur.

Molecule of sulfur trioxide

Water molecule

The atoms in the substances separate and combine with each other to form a molecule of sulfuric acid (H_2SO_4).

Molecule of sulfuric acid

These unusual formations at Mono Lake in California, USA, are called tufa towers. They are formed when a chemical reaction takes place between carbonates in the lake water and calcium from spring water (the reactants). The product is calcium carbonate, or limestone.

LAW OF CONSERVATION OF MASS

Matter cannot be created or destroyed during a chemical reaction. This is the **law of conservation of mass**. (Mass is the amount of matter a substance contains.)

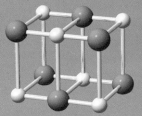

During a reaction between iron and sulfur, the atoms in the substances rearrange themselves.

Iron sulfide

After the reaction there is the same number of atoms and there is therefore the same amount of matter.

CHEMICAL EQUATIONS

Chemical reactions can be written as **equations** using the chemical formulae of the substances. In an equation, the reactants are written on the left and the products are written on the right. They are separated by an arrow. Because of the law of conservation of mass, both sides of an equation balance: the reactants and the products contain the same number of atoms.

This equation shows how hydrogen and oxygen react to form water. Both sides of the equation have the same number of atoms.

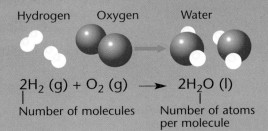

Hydrogen   Oxygen   Water

$$2H_2 (g) + O_2 (g) \longrightarrow 2H_2O (l)$$

Number of molecules

Number of atoms per molecule

Equations may also show the physical states of the substances involved in the reaction (**g** for gas, **l** for liquid, **s** for solid and **aq** for aqueous, that is, dissolved in water). If a catalyst* is used, it is shown above the arrow.

MOLES

Chemists measure chemical substances in **moles**. One mole is 602,300 million trillion molecules or atoms. This can be written as 6.023×10^{23} and is called the **Avogadro number**. It is the number of atoms found in a mass of 12g of carbon-12. A mole of a different element will have a different mass, but the same number of particles. A mole of magnesium has a mass of 24g because magnesium atoms weigh twice as much as carbon atoms.

A mole of magnesium has a mass of 24g.

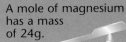

A mole of carbon has a mass of 12g.

See for yourself

To produce an exothermic reaction, mix plaster of Paris with water. You will notice that the mixture becomes warm.

This is because plaster of Paris is made by heating gypsum (hydrated* calcium sulfate) until it loses some of its water and becomes a powder. When water is added, it bonds again with the plaster to produce solid gypsum and heat.

Internet links

Go to **www.usborne-quicklinks.com** for links to the following Web sites:

Web site 1 Make a safe and controlled explosive reaction and launch your own rocket.

Web site 2 Play a game about balancing equations.

Web site 3 Basic information about chemical reactions.

Web site 4 Find out more information about moles.

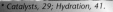

* Catalysts, 29; Hydration, 41.

TYPES OF REACTIONS

All chemical reactions either give off or take in energy. In **endothermic reactions**, energy is absorbed in the form of heat. For instance, when sherbet reacts with moisture on your tongue, heat is taken from your tongue, making it feel cool.

Any reactions that give off heat energy are **exothermic reactions**. (Combustion, also called burning, is one example of an exothermic reaction.) Your body feels warm because of exothermic reactions which are happening inside you all the time.

Some reactions take in or give off energy in the form of light rather than heat. These are called **photochemical reactions**. Plants take in light energy from sunlight. This enables them to make food, as part of a process called photosynthesis*.

These plants are taking energy from sunlight and making food in a photochemical reaction.

Synthesis reactions (also called **combination reactions**) involve substances combining to make a single new substance. For example, when magnesium is heated, it combines with oxygen in the air to produce a white ash called magnesium oxide.

Neutralization reactions take place when one substance reacts with another and each cancels out the other's properties. This is what happens when acids and alkalis are mixed. (See *Bases and Alkalis*, page 35.)

Reactions where a single substance breaks down into simpler substances are called **decomposition reactions**. When food rots, many of these reactions take place.

When heat is needed to break down a compound, the reaction is called a **thermal decomposition reaction**. For example, when limestone (calcium carbonate) is heated, it breaks down to form quicklime (calcium oxide) and carbon dioxide.

Heating limestone causes it to break down into different substances.

Reversible reactions are reactions in which the products, given the right conditions, react together to form the original reactants once again. Reactions of this type can be written as an equation. A symbol indicates that the reaction is reversible:

$$2NO_2 \rightleftharpoons 2NO + O_2$$

Nitrogen dioxide (NO_2) splits to produce nitrogen monoxide (NO) and oxygen (O_2). As they cool, they recombine to give nitrogen dioxide.

The first part of the reaction is called the **forward reaction**. The second part is called the **reverse reaction**.

Displacement reactions occur when a more reactive substance displaces a less reactive one. For example, when an iron nail is placed in copper(II) sulfate solution, the iron "pulls" the copper out of the solution and takes its place in the solution. The copper collects around the nail. The more reactive element (iron) displaces the less reactive copper.

Copper(II) sulfate solution

Copper on iron nail

RATES OF REACTION

Some chemical reactions, such as rusting, take place slowly over a long period of time. Others, such as the chemical reaction that takes place when gunpowder explodes, are almost instantaneous.

The rate of a reaction is affected by the **reactivity** of the substances. Very reactive elements react more quickly than less reactive elements.

During a chemical reaction, the atoms of the different substances must come into contact with each other in order to form new bonds. This happens more easily in gases and liquids, in which molecules are free to move around, so they tend to be more reactive than solid substances.

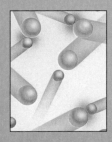

Heating substances increases the rate of a reaction. The heat makes more of the particles move fast enough to collide and react.

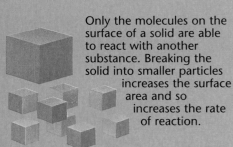

Only the molecules on the surface of a solid are able to react with another substance. Breaking the solid into smaller particles increases the surface area and so increases the rate of reaction.

When rainwater hits limestone, a chemical reaction occurs. The rainwater slowly dissolves the limestone to form carbonic acid. This eats away the limestone further.

CATALYSTS

Catalysts are substances that can change the rate of a chemical reaction, but are themselves left unchanged. Some catalysts speed up reactions while others, called **inhibitors**, slow them down.

Catalysts work by lowering the activation energy* of a reaction. They make it easier for the reaction to take place.

Metals are often used as catalysts. For example, **catalytic converters**, which remove toxic gases from car exhaust fumes, use metal catalysts, as shown below.

How a catalytic converter works

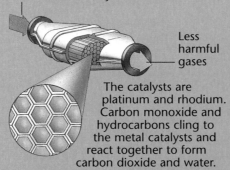

Exhaust fumes containing carbon monoxide and hydrocarbons.

Less harmful gases

The catalysts are platinum and rhodium. Carbon monoxide and hydrocarbons cling to the metal catalysts and react together to form carbon dioxide and water.

See for yourself

Here you can see how to make use of an exothermic reaction to reveal something written in invisible ink.

Dip a fine paintbrush in lemon juice and write a message on a piece of paper. Leave it to dry until it is invisible. To reveal the message, place the paper face down on a shelf in the oven and leave it there for ten minutes at 300°F.

The heat of the oven causes the lemon juice to burn – an exothermic reaction which makes the writing go brown. The heat is not enough, though, to burn the paper.

ENZYMES

Many chemical reactions that take place in living things are speeded up by catalysts called **enzymes**.

Enzymes, and many other catalysts, are **action specific**, that is, each speeds up only one type of reaction. Many different enzymes in the digestive systems of animals, including humans, help speed up the chemical reactions that break complex foods into simpler substances.

The picture shows the three main areas of your digestive system where enzymes work on your food.

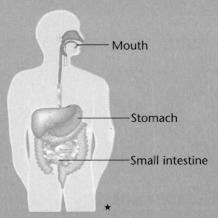

Mouth

Stomach

Small intestine

★

Internet links

Go to **www.usborne-quicklinks.com** for links to the following Web sites:

Web site 1 Try out an exothermic reaction.

Web site 2 Find out rates of reaction.

Web site 3 Learn more about catalysts.

Web site 4 Read about chemical reactions in garlic.

Web site 5 Learn how an internal combustion engine works using a chemical reaction.

Web site 6 Try an experiment to see the effect of surface area on the rate of reaction.

Web site 7 Read about the chemical reactions that take place in bread making.

* Activation energy, 26.

OXIDATION AND REDUCTION

Oxidation and reduction are terms which describe two types of chemical reactions. Unless specific conditions prevent it, these two reactions always occur together, in what are described as **redox reactions**. In a redox reaction, when one substance is oxidized, the other is reduced. For example, when wood burns, it is oxidized, while the air around it is reduced.

OXIDATION

The term **oxidation** describes reactions in which a substance combines with oxygen. This comes from another substance, called the **oxidizing agent** (which itself is reduced). For example, when iron is exposed to damp air, it slowly combines with oxygen in the air, forming hydrated iron oxide (rust).

Rusting (the corrosion of iron) is an oxidation reaction.

| Iron | Damp air | Rust |

Oxidation also describes reactions in which a substance loses hydrogen or electrons to another substance (the oxidizing agent). For example, when magnesium and chlorine combine to form magnesium chloride, magnesium loses two electrons (see *Ionic Bonding*, page 20). It is oxidized.

The magnesium atom loses two electrons to the chlorine atoms, and is oxidized.

Magnesium atom

Two chlorine atoms

INTERNAL RESPIRATION

Internal respiration, the process by which animals and plants break down glucose to release energy, is an oxidation reaction. In fact, it is a slow form of combustion (see below). This is the equation for internal respiration:

$$C_6H_{12}O_6 + 6O_2 \rightarrow 6CO_2 + 6H_2O$$

Glucose + Oxygen → Carbon dioxide + Water

COMBUSTION

Combustion (burning) is an oxidation reaction that gives off energy in the form of heat. When a substance burns, it combines with oxygen to form an oxide. Most fuels, for example, wood, gas and gasoline, contain hydrogen and carbon. Both these substances oxidize to produce water and carbon dioxide when they burn.

We now burn so much fuel for energy that the level of carbon dioxide in the air is increasing. Scientists think that the amount of combustion may be causing changes in the weather (see *Greenhouse Effect*, page 15).

The colors in fireworks come from the combustion of different elements. Strontium burns to give red sparks, copper gives blue and magnesium brilliant white.

Gasoline burning inside a motorcycle's engine is an example of combustion.

REDUCTION

During **reduction**, a substance loses oxygen to, or gains hydrogen or electrons from, another substance (the **reducing agent**, which is oxidized). For example, when copper oxide reacts with carbon, the copper oxide loses oxygen to the carbon, as shown below.

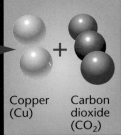
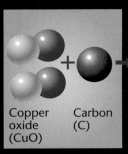

| Copper oxide (CuO) | Carbon (C) | Copper (Cu) | Carbon dioxide (CO$_2$) |

In this reaction, the copper oxide is reduced to pure copper by carbon, and the carbon is oxidized to form carbon dioxide.

$$2CuO + C \rightarrow CO_2 + 2Cu$$

Copper oxide + Carbon → Carbon dioxide + Copper

IRON SMELTING

The iron production process, called **smelting**, produces pure iron from iron ore. It is an example of a useful redox reaction.

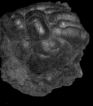

Iron ore

Inside a blast furnace, carbon is used to reduce iron ore (iron oxide) to pure iron. The carbon pulls oxygen away from (reduces) the ore. The carbon itself oxidizes to become carbon dioxide.

See for yourself

When a chunk of apple is left for a few minutes, it begins to turn brown. This is because chemicals on the apple's flesh take part in an oxidation reaction, using oxygen from the surrounding air. If you cover the apple with plastic food wrap, you stop the air from reacting with the apple, so it doesn't go brown.

PHOTOSYNTHESIS

Photosynthesis, the process by which plants make their food, is a reduction reaction. In photosynthesis, plants build glucose ($C_6H_{12}O_6$) from carbon dioxide and water, using energy from sunlight. Photosynthesis is the opposite of internal respiration (see opposite page). This is the equation for photosynthesis:

$$6CO_2 + 6H_2O \rightarrow C_6H_{12}O_6 + 6O_2$$

Carbon dioxide + Water → Glucose + Oxygen

This tulip plant feeds itself with the glucose it makes during photosynthesis.

Plants produce oxygen when they are photosynthesizing. They use some of it for internal respiration and the rest goes back into the air.

Internet links

Go to **www.usborne-quicklinks.com** for links to the following Web sites:

Web site 1 A thorough, step-by-step explanation of oxidation and reduction.

Web site 2 Find out about the chemistry of fireworks.

Web site 3 Learn the basics of oxidation and reduction, with definitions.

Web site 4 Find out about different types of fire extinguishers in the UK.

Web site 5 Read about different types of fire extinguishers in the USA.

ELECTROLYSIS

Electrolysis is a method of separating the elements in a compound by passing an electric current through the compound when it is molten or in a solution. The process is used to separate very reactive metals from their ores and to purify metals. It is also used to coat objects with a thin layer of metal in a process called electroplating.

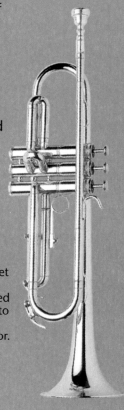

The nib of this pen has been plated with a thin layer of gold by electrolysis.

HOW ELECTROLYSIS WORKS

Only ionic compounds* can conduct electricity during electrolysis. This is because the particles that make up an ionic compound, called ions, have an electrical charge. Some of the particles (called anions) are negatively charged. Others (called cations) are positively charged.

During electrolysis, the ionic compound is called the **electrolyte**. An electric current is carried to it by two **electrodes**. One electrode (the **anode**) carries a positive charge. The other (the **cathode**) carries a negative charge.

ELECTROPLATING

Electroplating uses electrolysis to cover objects with a thin layer of metal. The object that is to be plated is used as a cathode and during electrolysis it becomes coated with metal from the electrolyte.

In industry, electroplating is used to protect cheap but reactive metals with a layer of less reactive metal. For example, steel is plated with tin or chromium to prevent rusting.

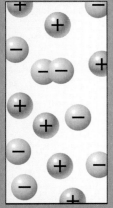

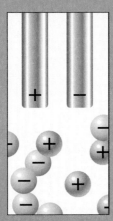

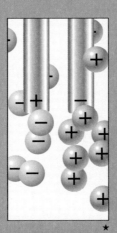

Copper(II) chloride solution can be used as an electrolyte. It is made up of positively charged copper cations and negatively charged chloride anions.

To carry the current, two electrodes, attached to an electric source, are placed in the compound. Nothing happens until the electric current flows.

As the electric current flows, the cations flow to the negative electrode where they gain electrons. The anions rush to the positive electrode and lose electrons.

These steel food cans have been plated with a very fine layer of tin to prevent rust.

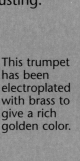

This trumpet has been electroplated with brass to give a rich golden color.

ELECTROREFINING

Electrorefining purifies metals by electrolysis. To purify copper, impure copper is used as an anode and pure copper as a cathode. A solution of copper(II) sulfate is used as an electrolyte.

Copper ions in the solution are attracted to the cathode. They are replaced in the solution by copper ions which split off from the anode, leaving the impurities behind.

Electrorefining copper

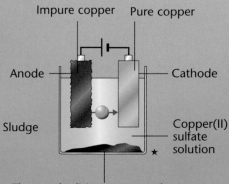

The anode disintegrates as the copper ions split off. Its impurities fall off, forming a sludge.

ANODIZING

Electrolysis can be used to coat some metals, such as aluminum, with a thin layer of their oxide (the compound it forms when it reacts with oxygen). This is called **anodizing**. The oxide forms a protective layer that prevents corrosion of the metal.

When anodizing aluminum, the object is used as the anode and placed in a solution of sulfuric acid, which is the electrolyte.

Oxide ions from the electrolyte collect at the anode and they react with the aluminum to form a layer of aluminum oxide.

METAL EXTRACTION

Very reactive metals, such as aluminum, are extracted from impure forms by electrolysis.

Aluminum is mined as **bauxite**, which is mainly aluminum oxide. For electrolysis, aluminum oxide is dissolved in cryolite to allow the ions to move. A graphite-lined tank forms the cathode. Aluminum ions are attracted to the cathode and become atoms of molten aluminum.

Extracting aluminum

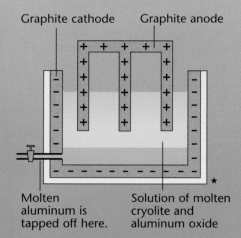

Graphite cathode — Graphite anode

Molten aluminum is tapped off here.

Solution of molten cryolite and aluminum oxide

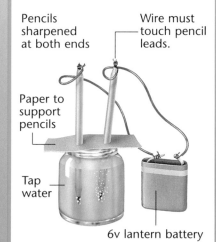

Anodized aluminum water flasks

The handlebars on this mountain bike are made of anodized aluminum that has been dyed blue.

See for yourself

You can use electrolysis to split water, which is a compound of hydrogen and oxygen, into bubbles of hydrogen and oxygen gas. Set up the equipment as shown below.

Pencils sharpened at both ends

Wire must touch pencil leads.

Paper to support pencils

Tap water

6v lantern battery

When you attach the wires to the battery, bubbles of hydrogen rush to the pencil attached to the negative battery terminal (cathode) because hydrogen forms positive ions. The bubbles on the other pencil, attached to the positive terminal, or anode, are oxygen. There are more hydrogen bubbles because each molecule of water (H_2O) contains two atoms of hydrogen but only one of oxygen.

Internet links

Go to **www.usborne-quicklinks.com** for links to the following Web sites:

Web site 1 Do an experiment to see whether a salt water solution can conduct electricity.

Web site 2 Find out how the Oscar statuettes are made and electroplated.

Web site 3 Read about fuel cells, and how they may be used one day to power electric cars.

Web site 4 Find out more about how fuel cells work.

Web site 5 Detailed information about electrolytes.

ACIDS AND BASES

The word acid comes from the Latin word *acer*, which means "sour". Acids contained in some foods make the food taste sour. For example, citrus fruits such as lemons, limes, oranges and grapefruits contain citric acid and ascorbic acid. The chemical opposite of an acid is a base. (A substance that is neither an acid nor a base is neutral.)

A bee's stinger contains an acid. It can be neutralized with soap, which is an alkali.

ACIDS

Hydrogen

Chlorine

Acids are compounds that contain hydrogen and which dissolve in water to produce hydrogen ions (H^+). Ions are particles that have an electrical charge. The hydrogen ions give acids their special properties, but they only exist in solution, so an acid only displays its properties when it is dissolved.

Hydrochloric acid (HCl) is made from hydrogen and chlorine.

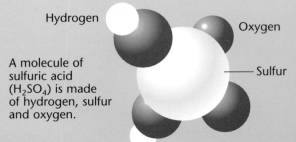

Hydrogen

Oxygen

Sulfur

A molecule of sulfuric acid (H_2SO_4) is made of hydrogen, sulfur and oxygen.

A **strong acid** is one in which most of the molecules separate to form a large number of hydrogen ions when it is in solution. Hydrochloric, sulfuric and nitric acid are all strong acids.

Strong acids are very **corrosive**. This means that they will burn your skin or the surface of an object.

The containers of strong acids are marked with the international warning symbols shown below, which mean corrosive (left) and harmful (right).

Corrosive

Harmful

ORGANIC ACIDS

Acids that are produced by living things, such as citric acid and ethanoic acid, are called **organic acids**. These are examples of **weak acids** (they contain few hydrogen ions). There is more about organic acids on page 44.

The colorful markings on the skin of sea slugs contain acids that taste horrible. This discourages predators from eating them.

Vinegar, which can be made from grapes, contains a weak acid called ethanoic acid.

Ants that can sting contain an acid called methanoic (or formic) acid.

Tomatoes contain an organic acid called salicylic acid.

HOW ACIDS BEHAVE

Acids react in certain ways with other substances. For example, they react with most metals to form salts and hydrogen gas. They also react with carbonates to give a salt, carbon dioxide gas and water.

BASES AND ALKALIS

A **base** is the chemical opposite of an acid. A base that can dissolve in water is called an **alkali**. When a base is mixed with an acid, it **neutralizes** (cancels out) the properties of the acid and the reaction produces a salt plus water.

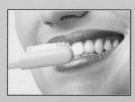

Toothpaste is a base that neutralizes the acids made in your mouth.

Indigestion tablets contain alkalis that neutralize the acids produced by the stomach.

When this wasp stings, it injects an alkali into its victim. If you get stung, you can neutralize the sting with vinegar (an acid).

Bases neutralize acids because they contain negative ions, which cancel out the positive hydrogen ions. The oxide ion (O^{2-}) and the hydroxide ion (OH^-) are both negative, so metal oxides, such as magnesium oxide, and metal hydroxides, such as sodium hydroxide (caustic soda), are bases.

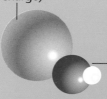

Sodium ion (positive charge)

Hydroxide ion (negative charge) cancels out sodium's positive charge, producing a base.

Magnesium ion (positive charge)

Hydroxide ions (negative charge) cancel out magnesium's positive charge, producing a base.

USING BASES

Many bases and alkalis can be very dangerous as they are **caustic** (dissolve the flesh). Liquid floor cleaners contain alkalis, such as ammonium hydroxide, that dissolve dirt. Sodium hydroxide is used in paper-making to dissolve the resin in wood, leaving the natural fibers of cellulose that are used to make paper.

Sodium hydroxide is also used to make oven cleaners, and mixed with potassium hydroxide to make soap.

See for yourself

To see how an acid and a base react together, pour some vinegar into a glass and add some bicarbonate of soda.

Bicarbonate of soda is a base. It reacts with ethanoic acid in the vinegar to produce sodium ethanoate (a salt), water and carbon dioxide.

As the substances mix, carbon dioxide bubbles out.

Internet links

Go to **www.usborne-quicklinks.com** for links to the following Web sites:

Web site 1 An introduction to acids and bases.

Web site 2 In-depth information about acids.

Web site 3 Try a simple experiment with an acid.

Web site 4 Browse a helpful list of questions and answers about acids and bases.

Web site 5 Read about papermaking.

pH NUMBERS

The strength of an acid or base can be expressed as a **pH number**. pH stands for "power of hydrogen" and is a measure of the concentration of hydrogen ions in a solution. pH values generally range between 0 and 14. The lower the pH number, the greater the concentration of hydrogen ions. A solution with a pH value of less than 7 is an acid. Substances with a pH value of 7 are neutral and those with pH values higher than 7 are bases or alkalis.

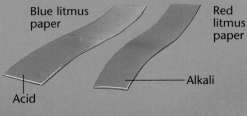

Orange juice has a pH value of 4, so it is a weak acid.

This wasp's stinger is a weak alkali with a pH of 9.

INDICATORS

An **indicator** can show whether something is an acid or an alkali. An indicator is a substance that changes color when it is placed in an acid or an alkali. One indicator, called **litmus**, turns red in an acid and blue in an alkali.

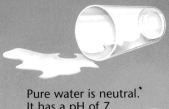

Blue litmus paper

Red litmus paper

Acid

Alkali

Acids turn blue litmus paper red.
Alkalis turn red litmus paper blue.

Litmus is an extract from plant-like organisms called lichens. Some plants, for example hydrangeas and red cabbage, are also natural indicators. Another indicator, called **universal indicator**, is a mixture of several dyes that change color according to the pH scale, as shown in the picture below.

Paper strips containing universal indicator change color when they touch an acid or alkali. The numbers beside each color show the pH value.

Pure water is neutral.
It has a pH of 7.

Sodium hydroxide, used in household cleaners, is a strong alkali with a pH of 13.

1 2 3 4 5 6 7 8 9 10 11 12 13 14

ACIDS IN THE SOIL

The acidity of the soil depends on the type of rocks from which it is formed and the plants that grow in it. In chalk or limestone areas, the soil is usually alkaline, but in moorlands, sandstone and forested areas, it is more acidic. Acid rain* also adds to the acidity of the soil. Neutral or slightly acid soils with pH values of 6.5 to 7 are the best for farming.

In areas where the soil is too acidic, it can be improved by adding limestone (calcium carbonate) or slaked lime (calcium hydroxide). These are bases that neutralize the acidity.

Some plants, such as azaleas and rhododendrons, grow well in acid soil. Plants such as hydrangeas have blue flowers in acid soils and pink ones in alkaline soils.

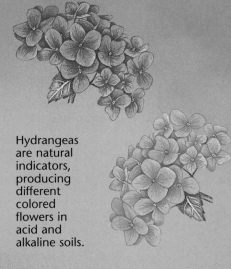

Hydrangeas are natural indicators, producing different colored flowers in acid and alkaline soils.

When leaves die and decompose, they form an acid called humic acid, which adds to the acidity of the soil.

* Acid rain, 15.

SULFURIC ACID

Sulfuric acid (H_2SO_4) is a chemical used in many different industries. Its main use is in the production of superphosphates and ammonium sulfate for fertilizers. Sulfuric acid is also used in car batteries, and in the manufacture of some synthetic fibers (such as rayon), dyes, plastics, drugs, explosives and detergents.

Sulfuric acid is used in the production of titanium oxide, a pigment used to make colored paint such as this.

Sulfuric acid is a type of **mineral acid**. Mineral acids are made from elements (in this case, sulfur) found as minerals in the Earth's crust.

Here you can see yellow crystals of sulfur produced by a volcano. Sulfur can be collected from volcanic areas and used in the manufacture of sulfuric acid.

Concentrated sulfuric acid is very reactive and highly corrosive. It produces lots of heat when dissolved in water and must always be added to the water, not the other way around. That way, the acid is rapidly diluted and the heat is absorbed by the water.

Concentrated sulfuric acid is a powerful oxidizing agent (it gives oxygen to other substances during oxidation*). It is also a **dehydrating agent** (it removes water that is chemically combined in another substance).

Sugar

Sulfuric acid

Carbon   Water

When sugar is warmed with concentrated sulfuric acid, the acid removes water from the sugar, leaving a foamy mass of black carbon and water.

* Oxidation, 30.

SALTS

In chemical terms, compounds made of a metal and a non-metal bonded together are **salts**. Many salts occur naturally in the Earth's crust and under the right conditions they form beautiful crystals. Salts have many different uses. For example, anhydrous calcium sulfate, also called **plaster of Paris**, is a salt used in decorative moldings, model-making and to make protective casts for broken limbs.

Here, plaster of Paris, a salt that sets hard when it is mixed with water, is being used to make a cast of an animal track.

WHAT IS A SALT?

Salts are ionic compounds*, that is, they are made up of ions (particles with an electric charge). Most salts form into regular crystal structures.

Salts are made when the hydrogen ions in an acid are replaced by a metal. For example, when hydrochloric acid and sodium hydroxide (an alkali) react together, sodium replaces the acid's hydrogen ions, creating sodium chloride (a salt) and water. (See picture, above right.)

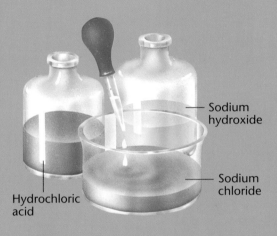

Sodium hydroxide

Sodium chloride

Hydrochloric acid

In the picture above, each ingredient of the experiment has had litmus added to it to show whether it is an acid or a base.

SALT FAMILIES

There are several families of salts made with different acids. **Sulfates** are made with sulfuric acid, **chlorides** are made with hydrochloric acid, **nitrates** are made with nitric acid and **carbonates** with carbonic acid.

Bath salts and washing soda (water softener) are sodium carbonate. They react with magnesium and calcium salts in hard water* to form insoluble particles of calcium carbonate.

Soluble salts are those, such as washing soda, that dissolve in water to form a solution. **Insoluble salts** are ones that do not dissolve in water. Limestone and chalk are made of calcium carbonate, which is an insoluble salt.

Vermilion red

Malachite green

Cadmium yellow

The salts vermilion, cadmium sulfide and malachite are used to make artists' paints.

SODIUM CHLORIDE

Sodium chloride (**NaCl**) is the chemical name for common salt. It is a soluble salt. A concentrated solution of sodium chloride in water is called **brine**.

Sodium chloride can be extracted from sea water by evaporation, and it is also found in solid form as **rock salt**, or **halite**. It is used to flavor and preserve food and is essential to animal life.

Sodium chloride is an important raw material and it is used in the manufacture of hydrochloric acid, chlorine, sodium hydroxide (caustic soda) and sodium carbonate (washing soda). It is sprinkled on roads in winter because it lowers the freezing point of water and stops ice from forming.

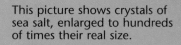

This picture shows crystals of sea salt, enlarged to hundreds of times their real size.

MAKING SALTS

There are several ways to make salts in the laboratory. Soluble salts can be made by reacting an acid and a metal, or metal oxide (a base).

Copper(II) sulfate is made by adding copper oxide to dilute sulfuric acid.

Copper oxide

The mixture is then filtered. The filtrate is a solution of copper(II) sulfate. Unused copper oxide is left in the filter paper.

Filtrate

The solution is heated to remove water, then left to form crystals of copper(II) sulfate.

★

Insoluble salts are made from two soluble salts that react together to form a **precipitate** (insoluble solid particles) of salt in a solution. The solution is then filtered to remove the precipitate. Salts can also be made by combining two elements. For example, iron sulfide is made by heating iron with sulfur (see page 16).

FERTILIZERS

Fertilizers are nutrients that help plants to grow. Many fertilizers contain salts, such as nitrates, phosphates and potash, that are soluble in water and can be absorbed by plants' roots. Nitrates contain nitrogen, phosphates contain phosphorus, and potash contains potassium salts. All of these are needed for healthy plant growth.

The smaller plant shown here was grown in poor soil. The larger one was grown in fertilized soil.

See for yourself

Crystals of table salt contain water (see *Hydration*, page 41), but you can turn them powdery just by leaving them on a plate for a few days.

When you leave the crystals in the air the water escapes, leaving a dry powder. Similarly, if you leave the lid off a bottle of bath crystals, these also lose their shape and turn powdery.

Internet links

Go to **www.usborne-quicklinks.com** for links to the following Web sites:

Web site 1 Find lots of information about sodium chloride (table salt).

Web site 2 A photo gallery containing some fantastic images of salts, as seen through an electron microscope.

Web site 3 Find out about the role played by salts, such as alum, in the wool dyeing process.

Web site 4 Find out about halite, also known as rock salt (the mineral form of sodium chloride), with information and images relating to other mineral salts.

CRYSTALS

When allowed to form slowly, salts and many other substances form crystals. A **crystal** is a solid that has a definite geometrical shape with straight edges and flat surfaces. Most solids, even metals, are made up of crystals but they are so small that you cannot see them. Some of the minerals in the Earth's crust form beautiful crystals, such as diamonds and emeralds.

Pyrite (also called iron pyrites or fools' gold) is a common mineral made of iron and sulfur. Its crystals are often cubic in shape.

HOW CRYSTALS FORM

Some substances form crystals as they cool and solidify. Others crystallize when the water in which they were dissolved evaporates. The shape of the crystals depends on the regular arrangement and bonding of the particles in the substance. Different substances form different shaped crystals. The main crystal shapes are shown in the picture below.

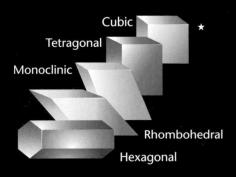

Cubic
Tetragonal
Monoclinic
Rhombohedral
Hexagonal

Calcite crystals can be ground up to make cement.

SPLITTING CRYSTALS

The boundaries between the particles in a crystal are called **cleavage planes**. Crystals split along these planes, leaving the flat surfaces of the crystal exposed. If a crystal is not split along a cleavage plane, it will shatter.

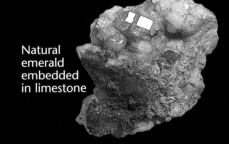

Natural emerald embedded in limestone

The emerald set in this ring has been split along its cleavage planes to make a beautiful gem.

Amethyst crystals form from the mineral quartz.

LIQUID CRYSTALS

Liquid crystals are crystals that become cloudy when heated. They are used in **liquid crystal displays** (**LCDs**) in watches, calculators and televisions.

When an electric current is passed through the crystals, their molecules line up and block the light, creating the pattern of the display. LCD TV screens contain many thousands of tiny crystal units. They build up the moving pictures that you see by flashing on and off very quickly.

This handheld digital television has a liquid crystal display.

Crystals of apatite. This substance is also found in teeth.

HYDRATION

Hydration occurs when a substance combines with water. The substance is said to be **hydrated**. Many salts combine and chemically bond with water to form crystals. The water is then known as **water of crystallization**.

Hydrated copper(II) sulfate crystals ($CuSO_4.5H_2O$) form when copper(II) sulfate ($CuSO_4$) bonds with water (H_2O).

This crystal is halite. It was formed by the evaporation of sea water thousands of years ago.

In a crystal, the water is chemically bonded with the atoms of the substance, unlike in a solution where the atoms of the substance are mixed but not bonded with the molecules of water. Water can be made to separate from a hydrated solid by heating the solid. This is called **dehydration**.

If you heat washing soda ($Na_2CO_3.10H_2O$) crystals, the water of crystallization separates off, and a solution of washing soda is formed.

Dehydration can also be carried out using a **dehydrating agent**, such as sulfuric acid.

The dry solid which results from dehydration is said to be **anhydrous**.

White, anhydrous copper(II) sulfate powder turns blue when water is added. It can be used to test for the presence of water.

See for yourself

You can grow a crystal using **alum** (a sulfate of potassium and aluminum). It will take about three weeks to grow. You can buy alum from a pharmacy. Alum can be harmful if eaten, so remember to wash your hands after touching it.

1. Gently warm 100g of alum in 500ml of water over a low heat until it dissolves, then add more alum until no more will dissolve.

2. Pour a little of this saturated solution into a saucer and leave it for three days. Keep the rest of the solution in a clean, covered jar.

3. When crystals appear on the saucer, tie a thread around one and suspend it in the solution in the jar. This crystal is called the **seed crystal**. The solution will slowly crystallize around it.

Seed crystal on saucer

QUARTZ CRYSTALS

Quartz crystals are crystals of the mineral quartz that form in the Earth's crust. When a current of electricity is passed through a quartz crystal, it vibrates 32,768 times a second. This is called the **piezoelectric effect**. The vibrations can be used to measure time in clocks and watches.

Quartz crystals inside a watch are often shaped into two prongs. The current from the watch battery makes them vibrate.

Internet links

Go to **www.usborne-quicklinks.com** for links to the following Web sites:

Web site 1 Choose from hundreds of minerals, each with its own picture and details of its physical properties, classification and more.

Web site 2 More about crystals, including recipes, facts and games.

Web site 3 Find lots of information about different crystal shapes, and how they form, then try growing your own crystals.

Web site 4 Discover why quartz crystals are used in watches.

Web site 5 See detailed information about the different types of cleavage planes.

ORGANIC CHEMISTRY

Organic chemistry is the study of compounds of carbon, called **organic compounds**. All living things contain organic compounds, and many can be made artificially. They are used to create fabrics, medicines, plastics, paints, cosmetics and many other products.

Paints contain organic compounds.

ORGANIC COMPOUNDS

Organic compounds are made up of carbon atoms bonded to atoms of other elements such as hydrogen and oxygen. The atoms are held together by strong covalent bonds (see right). Compounds that contain only carbon and hydrogen atoms are called **hydrocarbons**.

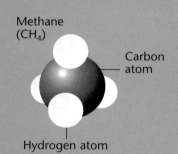

Methane (CH$_4$)

Carbon atom

Hydrogen atom

Organic compounds are grouped in families called **homologous series**. For example, alkanes and alkenes (see pages 46-47) are two homologous series. Each series contains hundreds of compounds, with increasing numbers of carbon and hydrogen atoms in their molecules.

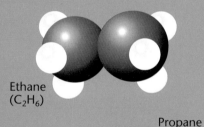

Ethane (C$_2$H$_6$)

Here are models of molecules of the first three compounds in the alkane series. **Methane** has one carbon atom, **ethane** has two and **propane** has three.

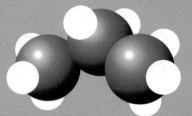

Propane (C$_3$H$_8$)

The names of compounds with molecules containing one carbon atom start with "meth". Those with molecules containing two carbon atoms start with "eth" and those with three carbon atoms begin with "prop". The compounds in each homologous series have the same chemical properties, but their physical properties change from gas to liquid to solid as the molecules increase in size.

The dyes used on these ballet shoes are made from an organic compound called **aniline**, which is found in coal tar.

COVALENT BONDS

Covalent bonds (see page 19) are the strong links between atoms that share electrons in their outer shells.

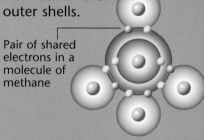

Pair of shared electrons in a molecule of methane

Each carbon atom can form single bonds with four other atoms, or it can form double, or even triple bonds. In **single bonds**, each pair of atoms shares one pair of electrons, in **double bonds** they share two and in **triple bonds** they share three pairs of electrons. In diagrams of organic molecules, the bonds are usually shown as sticks between the atoms.

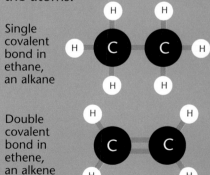

Single covalent bond in ethane, an alkane

Double covalent bond in ethene, an alkene

Carbon atoms can join together to form long chains or rings which makes a huge number of organic compounds possible.

UNSATURATED

Organic compounds with double or triple bonds are described as **unsaturated**. They have bonds that can open up and join with other atoms without the original molecules breaking up. When this happens, the type of reaction that takes place is called an **addition reaction**.

Unsaturated compounds are more reactive than saturated compounds (see right).

An addition reaction

When ethene reacts with bromine, its double bonds open up, making space for bromine atoms.

Ethene (C_2H_4)

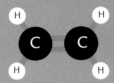

Bromine (Br_2)

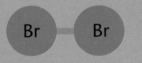

1,2-dibromoethane (CH_2BrCH_2Br)

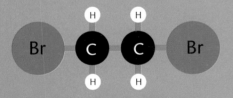

$$C_2H_4 + Br_2 \longrightarrow CH_2BrCH_2Br$$

Ethene and bromine react to form 1,2-dibromoethane, which is used in insecticides and rat poisons.

Tablet containers like these are called blister packs. They are made from artificial organic compounds such as PVC (polyvinylchloride).

SATURATED

Organic compounds with single bonds are said to be **saturated**, or "full", as they have no free bonds to join with other atoms.

When saturated organic compounds react with other compounds, the bonds in their molecules break open and some of their atoms are replaced by different atoms. This is called a **substitution reaction**. For example, dichlorodifluoromethane (CCl_2F_2) is made by replacing the hydrogen atoms in methane (CH_4) with chlorine (Cl) and fluorine (F).

$$CH_4 + 2Cl_2 + 2F_2 \longrightarrow CCl_2F_2 + 2HF + 2HCl$$

Aerosol propellants used to be made of dichlorodifluoromethane, but this is a chlorofluorocarbon (a chlorine-fluorine-carbon compound) and damages the atmosphere. Other propellants are now used in aerosols.

SYNTHETIC COMPOUNDS

By studying the way different organic compounds react, chemists have been able to synthesize (copy) substances that occur naturally, and make them in laboratories. Chemists have also created completely new, artificial organic compounds.

Chemists make vitamin tablets by synthesizing (copying) the structure of vitamins, which are naturally occurring organic compounds.

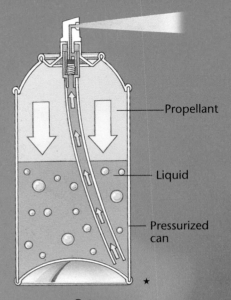

Propellant

Liquid

Pressurized can

★

Cutaway drawing of an aerosol spray-can.

Internet links

Go to **www.usborne-quicklinks.com** for links to the following Web sites:

Web site 1 A good source of interactive 3-D molecular models, including models of hydrocarbons.

Web site 2 Find lots of information about organic chemistry.

Web site 3 Advanced definition of organic chemistry terms.

Web site 4 An in-depth look at common organic chemistry reactions.

Web site 5 An online encyclopedia with a brief introduction to organic chemistry.

ALCOHOLS

Alcohols are organic compounds that contain carbon, oxygen and hydrogen. They are a **homologous series**, that is, a group of compounds with the same chemical properties.

The oxygen and hydrogen atoms in an alcohol molecule form a **hydroxyl group** that gives the alcohols their special properties.

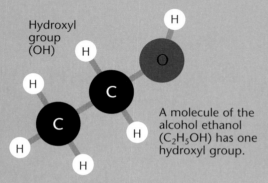

Hydroxyl group (OH)

A molecule of the alcohol ethanol (C_2H_5OH) has one hydroxyl group.

In industry, an alcohol called **ethanol** (C_2H_5OH) is made by fermentation (see below), or by reacting ethene (C_2H_4) with steam:

$$C_2H_4 + H_2O \longrightarrow C_2H_5OH$$

Ethanol is used as a solvent* for paints, varnishes and perfumes. Alcoholic drinks such as wine and beer contain ethanol.

FERMENTATION

Fermentation is a chemical reaction that has been used for thousands of years to produce alcoholic drinks. It is now an important industrial process for producing the alcohol ethanol.

Yeast, a fungus, causes fermentation. It produces **enzymes** – catalysts that speed up chemical reactions in living things. These convert the sugars in fruit or grain into ethanol and carbon dioxide.

ORGANIC ACIDS

Organic compounds that are acidic are called **organic acids**. They behave like typical acids, turning litmus paper red and forming salts when they react with bases.

Organic acids can be made by oxidizing (adding oxygen to) alcohols. Vinegar has been made for thousands of years by allowing wine, which contains the alcohol ethanol, to oxidize and form ethanoic acid.

TYPES OF ORGANIC ACID

Ethanoic acid, which gives vinegar its sour taste, and **methanoic acid**, the poison in the sting of some ants, are organic acids. They belong to a group called **carboxylic acids**.

Carboxylic acids contained in natural oils and fats are called **fatty acids**.

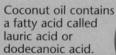

Coconut oil contains a fatty acid called lauric acid or dodecanoic acid.

This ant is about to squirt its poison of methanoic acid, a carboxylic acid.

Ethanoic acid is used in the manufacture of polyester. This can be spun very fine and dyed to make sewing threads.

DETERGENT

A **detergent** is a substance that enables water to remove dirt. Detergents reduce the attraction between the water molecules so the water spreads easily over the laundry. It is this loss of attraction between the molecules that allows stretchy bubbles to form on the water.

Without detergent, water molecules will not stretch apart very well. Any bubbles that form will pop within seconds.

Soap is a type of detergent made from vegetable oils, which contain fatty acids. When the oils are boiled with sodium hydroxide, an alkali, the acids react with the alkali to produce a salt, which is soap.

How detergents work

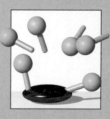

Detergents are made of ions* that have a charge at one end. This end is attracted to water. The other end (the tail) is attracted to grease.

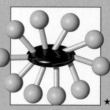

The tails attach themselves to grease and form a bridge between the water and the grease. Their attraction to water pulls the grease away from the laundry.

Soapless detergents work in the same way as soap. However, they are unaffected by the minerals in hard water*, which react with the soap to form a scum.

See for yourself

To see a detergent at work, sprinkle some talcum powder over the surface of a bowl of water. The talc will settle on the water's surface.

Now drip a drop of liquid dish detergent into the middle of the bowl and watch.

The detergent reduces the water's pulling power near where it lands, but not further away. As a result, the talc is pulled outward by the water with the greater pulling power.

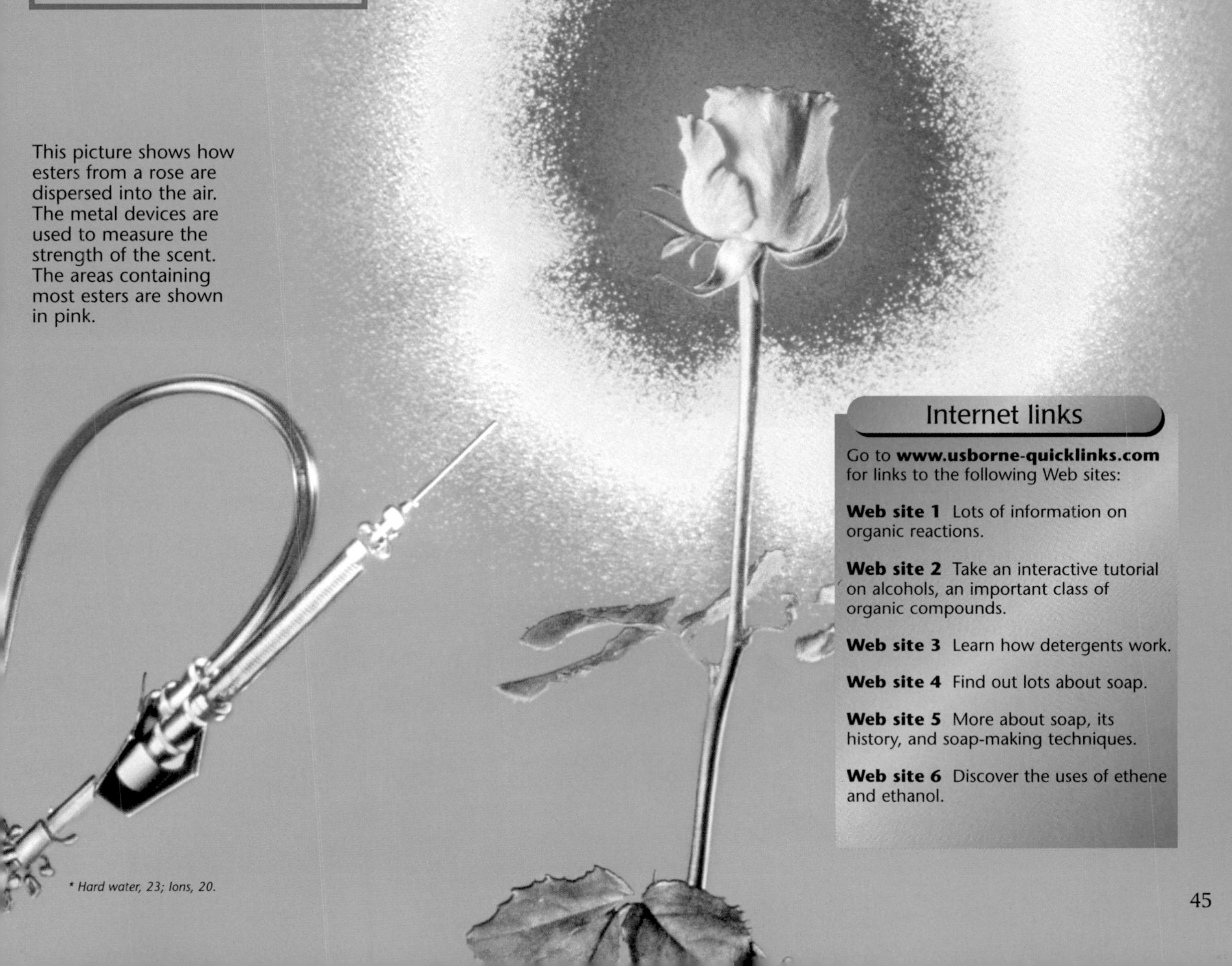

This picture shows how esters from a rose are dispersed into the air. The metal devices are used to measure the strength of the scent. The areas containing most esters are shown in pink.

ESTERS

When carboxylic acids react with alcohols, they produce compounds called **esters**, and water. Esters give fruit and flowers their flavors and smells. **Fats** and **oils** are esters made from propan-1,2,3-triol (an alcohol known as **glycerol**) combined with fatty acids.

Internet links

Go to **www.usborne-quicklinks.com** for links to the following Web sites:

Web site 1 Lots of information on organic reactions.

Web site 2 Take an interactive tutorial on alcohols, an important class of organic compounds.

Web site 3 Learn how detergents work.

Web site 4 Find out lots about soap.

Web site 5 More about soap, its history, and soap-making techniques.

Web site 6 Discover the uses of ethene and ethanol.

* Hard water, 23; Ions, 20.

ALKANES AND ALKENES

Alkanes are found in the Earth's crust in crude oil and natural gas, and many are used as fuels. Alkenes are not found naturally in great quantities and are obtained by breaking up large alkane molecules. They are both homologous series of hydrocarbons (see *Organic Compounds*, page 42).

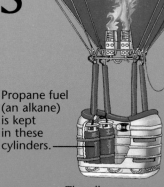

Propane fuel (an alkane) is kept in these cylinders.

The alkane propane is used as a fuel to heat the air in hot-air balloons.

ALKANES

Alkanes are a homologous series of saturated compounds. This means that their carbon atoms are held together by single covalent bonds*.

All alkane names end in "ane". Those with small molecules, such as methane, are gases, but those with larger ones are liquids. Alkanes with more than 16 carbon atoms are solids.

USES OF ALKANES

Alkanes burn easily and many are used as fuels. Gasoline is a mixture of alkanes, and propane and butane are used in mobile homes and camping stoves, stored under pressure as liquids in portable cylinders.

Alkanes are used to make many other organic chemicals. For example, the hydrogen atoms in methane can be replaced with chlorine and fluorine to make compounds called **chlorofluorocarbons** (**CFCs**). Many chlorofluorocarbons are no longer used, though, as they are thought to harm the atmosphere.

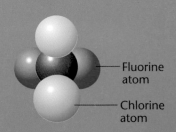

Fluorine atom

Chlorine atom

The molecule above is dichlorodifluoromethane, a CFC. It is used as a coolant in refrigerators, and in air conditioning systems for cars.

Methane, the main compound in natural gas, is used as a fuel for cooking and heating.

Aircraft use kerosene, a mixture of alkanes, for fuel. It is produced by the purification of petroleum.

Enormous amounts of fuel are used by jet planes. A Boeing 747 can carry nearly 57,000 gallons. It uses the fuel at a rate of about 5 gallons per mile.

Kerosene is an ideal fuel for a jet engine because, unlike some other fuels, it burns well in the freezing temperatures of high altitudes.

* Covalent bonds, 42.

ALKENES

Alkenes are a homologous series of hydrocarbons whose molecules contain some double covalent bonds (see page 43). The names of the compounds in this series end in "ene". Ethene (C_2H_4) is the first alkene. There is no alkene beginning with "meth" (see page 42) as all alkenes must have at least two carbon atoms to form a double bond.

The diagrams below show molecules of the first two compounds in the alkene series.

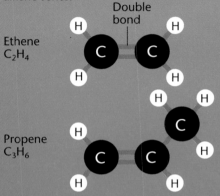

Ethene
C_2H_4

Double bond

Propene
C_3H_6

Alkenes are unsaturated* compounds and are more reactive than alkanes. Each carbon atom can give up one of its double bonds to other atoms in an addition reaction* without the molecules breaking open. Alkenes are used in industry to make plastics, such as polythene, by joining many molecules together.

Plastic clothespins. Plastics are manufactured by addition reactions, using molecules of compounds such as ethene.

Race cars are made of a very strong, rigid material called Kevlar®, which is plastic reinforced with synthetic fibers. It is much lighter than metal.

HYDROGENATION

Hydrogenation is an addition reaction* in which atoms of hydrogen are added to unsaturated* molecules, such as those of alkenes, to fill up the double covalent bonds. The new compounds are saturated* as they contain only single covalent bonds.

Ethene and hydrogen react together to form ethane. The hydrogen fills up the spare bonds in the double covalent bond.

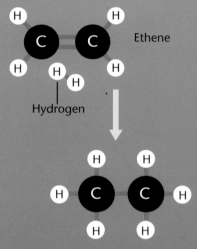

Ethene

Hydrogen

Ethane is an alkane and it is a saturated compound.

Food scientists use hydrogenation to make margarines from certain vegetable oils, such as olive oil. These oils contain alkenes.

Food scientists use hydrogenation to make margarines from certain vegetable oils, such as olive oil. These oils contain alkenes.

To create the margarine, hydrogen is forced through the oil while it is hot and pressurized. Some bonds break open and the hydrogen atoms attach to the newly available bonds. This causes the runny oil to become more solid.

Peanut oils consist of alkanes. They are used to make margarines.

The more hydrogenated vegetable oil becomes, the harder it is to spread.

See for yourself

Watch for advertisements for margarine. There is a strong chance that the manufacturers will claim that their product is the "healthy" alternative to butter.

This is because margarines contain more unsaturated compounds than butter (which consists mostly of saturated compounds).

Scientists think that saturated compounds are bad for you, since your body converts them into a type of cholesterol that can clog up your blood vessels. The unsaturated compounds in many margarines don't do this.

Internet links

Go to **www.usborne-quicklinks.com** for links to the following Web sites:

Web site 1 Find out about the physical and chemical properties of alkanes and alkenes.

Web site 2 A clear introduction to alkanes and alkenes.

Web site 3 An in-depth look at alkanes, including how they are named.

Web site 4 A detailed introduction to alkenes and how they are named.

Web site 5 Discover the types of fat found in food, and the difference between saturated and unsaturated fats.

Web site 6 Learn about naming organic compounds.

Web site 7 Take a quiz about naming organic compounds.

Addition reactions, Saturated, Unsaturated, 43.

CRUDE OIL

Crude oil is the raw material from which fuels such as heating oil, fuel and gas are obtained, as well as many different chemicals for industry. It is a mixture of hydrocarbons, which are organic compounds made only of carbon and hydrogen. The different compounds in the mixture are separated in oil refineries by a process called fractional distillation.

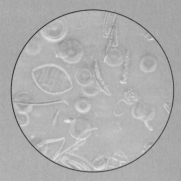

The microscopic organisms from which oil formed were similar to these plankton that live in the sea today.

HOW OIL AND GAS FORMED

Crude oil and natural gas are **fossil fuels**. They formed from the bodies of microscopic organisms that lived in the sea millions of years ago. When the organisms died, their bodies sank to the bottom of the sea and became buried in sand and mud. As the layers of sand and mud built up and became rock, the minute organisms rotted and formed oil and gas.

OIL FROM UNDER THE SEA

Nearly a third of all oil supplies are found under the seabed. The oil and gas are contained in pockets, called **reservoirs**, which are found in porous layers of rock. These reservoirs can be hundreds of feet below the seabed.

To extract the oil, giant oil platforms, like the one on the left, are built out at sea. Wells are drilled down from the seabed into the reservoirs. Oil is piped up to the platform from the reservoirs.

Oil platforms like this one are used to drill for deposits under the seabed.

Drill pipes

This picture shows four separate wells which have been drilled down from one platform.

Oil platform

Sea

Seabed

Well

Layers of rock

Oil reservoir

FRACTIONAL DISTILLATION

Fractional distillation is a process by which substances in a mixture can be separated by boiling. In an oil refinery, crude oil is heated until the compounds become gases at about 340°C. The gases are piped into a tower called a **fractionating column**. As they rise up the tower, they cool, condense (become liquids again) and are collected.

Fractionating columns at an oil refinery

The compounds with the largest, heaviest molecules condense first and are collected near the bottom of the tower. Compounds with smaller, lighter molecules have lower boiling points, so they rise higher up the tower before they condense. The mixture of compounds that condense at each level is called a **fraction**.

Fractionating column

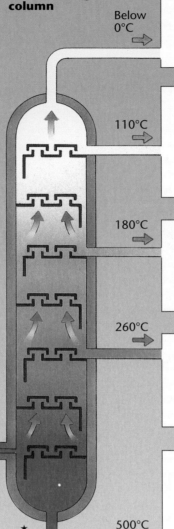

Furnace where crude oil is heated until it boils and the compounds become gases.

Below 0°C

110°C

180°C

260°C

500°C

Refinery gases
1-4 carbon atoms per molecule. Used as fuels for heating and cooking.

Gasoline compounds
5-12 carbon atoms per molecule. Used for gasoline and for making medicines, plastics, paints and chemicals.

Kerosene compounds
9-15 carbon atoms per molecule. Used for heating, lighting and jet fuels.

Diesel oils
12-25 carbon atoms per molecule. Used as fuels for trucks and trains.

Residue compounds
20-40 carbon atoms per molecule. Used for heating oil, candle waxes, polishes, lubricants and bitumen for surfacing roads.

CRACKING

Cracking is a method by which compounds with large molecules, such as decane, an alkane*, are converted to compounds with smaller molecules that are more useful and can be used as fuels or in the chemicals industry.

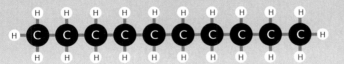
Decane (C$_{10}$H$_{22}$)

When heated and mixed with steam and a catalyst*, the large molecules break up to make smaller, lighter molecules.

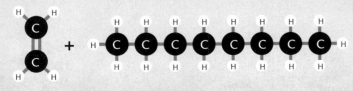
Ethene (C$_2$H$_4$)   +   Octane (C$_8$H$_{18}$)

Internet links

Go to **www.usborne-quicklinks.com** for links to the following Web sites:

Web site 1 Fascinating information about many aspects of crude oil.

Web site 2 Find out about modern methods of crude oil refining.

Web site 3 Read detailed information about crude oil distillation.

Web site 4 Find lots of useful information and animations related to hydrocarbons, the cracking process, and how oil deposits are formed.

* Alkanes, 46; Catalysts, 29.

POLYMERS AND PLASTICS

Polymers are substances made of many small molecules joined together to make long chains. Plastics and synthetic fibers, such as **nylon**, are polymers made from chemicals found in crude oil. As well as these synthetic polymers, there are natural polymers, such as rubber, starch, wool and silk – and the hair on your head.

Plastic balls are made by pouring molten polymers into a mold. As they cool, the shape solidifies.

MAKING PLASTICS

Plastics are easily-molded synthetic polymers made from the organic compounds found in crude oil. Many plastics, such as polythene, PVC and polystyrene, are made using ethene, which belongs to the group of organic compounds called alkenes*.

PVC drink bottles are light and shatterproof.

Polythene can be made into thin sheets for wrapping food.

Polythene and polystyrene can be molded to make things such as cups.

See for yourself

To make your own polymer, put a tablespoon of water in a cup with a teaspoon of egg white and a teaspoon of baking soda, and mix well. Then sprinkle a teaspoon of citric acid into the mixture and swirl it around.

The baking soda reacts with the citric acid, producing bubbles of carbon dioxide gas, turning the mixture into a foam. As this happens, monomers in the egg white bond together to form a polymer.

Don't eat the polymer – it may upset your stomach.

POLYMERIZATION

Joining molecules together to make polymers is called **polymerization**. The small molecules that make up polymers are called **monomers**.

For example, using heat, pressure and catalysts*, monomers of ethene are made to react together. Ethene has double bonds which open up and the carbon atoms join together to form long chains that are giant molecules of **polythene**.

Different plastics can be made by changing some of the atoms in the monomers. For example, by replacing a hydrogen atom in ethene with an atom of chlorine, chloroethene monomers are made. Long chains of these form **PVC** (polyvinylchloride).

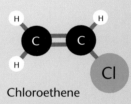
Chloroethene

Making polythene

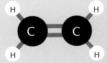

Each monomer of ethene (C_2H_4) contains two atoms of carbon joined by a double bond.

The double bond opens up to form bonds with other monomers to build the polymer.

A giant molecule of polythene contains up to 20,000 atoms of carbon.

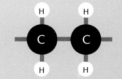

PVC is light, hardwearing and can be dyed easily. This juggling equipment makes use of all these qualities.

* Alkenes, 47; Catalysts, 29.

TYPES OF PLASTICS

Plastics can be divided into two groups. **Thermoplastics** can be melted and used again, while **thermosetting plastics** can be molded only once.

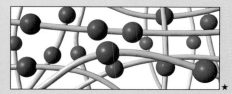

In thermoplastics, the polymer chains are not linked together.

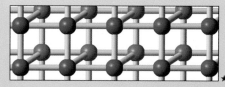

In thermosetting plastics the polymers are linked firmly together.

Thermoplastics are flexible but they are not heat resistant. Polythene, polystyrene, nylon and polyester fabrics are thermoplastics. These types of plastics are widely recycled.

Fibers for clothing can be made from recycled thermoplastics.

Thermosetting plastics have a rigid structure and are hard and heat resistant. Melamine, from which mugs, plates and kitchen work surfaces are made, is a thermosetting plastic.

Protective cases for electrical equipment, such as this drill, are often made from thermoplastics reinforced with glass fiber. They are strong, light and do not conduct electricity.

SYNTHETIC FIBERS

Some plastics can be drawn out to make fibers. Nylon, polyester and acrylic are three different types of plastics used to make fibers. They can be spun and woven, often together with natural fibers such as wool and cotton, to make clothes, carpets, ropes and strong fabrics for sails and parachutes.

This swimmer's costume is made from a strong, lightweight, flexible synthetic fiber. The material doesn't hold water, so it won't become heavy when wet.

Synthetic fibers are stronger and lighter than natural fibers such as wool and cotton. They can also be drawn out to make very long threads, unlike most natural fibers that have to be spun to make long lengths.

This picture shows a microscopic view of nylon fibers in a stocking. Nylon is a plastic made by reacting carboxylic acids and amine.

NATURAL POLYMERS

Not all polymers are synthetic. Before the invention of plastics, natural polymers such as wool and plant fibers (such as cotton and jute) were used for weaving. Like plastics, natural polymers are chains of simple molecules. The proteins in your body are also natural polymers.

Rubber is made from a natural polymer called **latex**, a milky fluid that seeps out of the bark of rubber trees. Rubber is strengthened by heating it with sulfur. This is called **vulcanized rubber** and is used mainly for making tires.

Latex is a natural polymer produced by rubber trees. It is collected in pots that are nailed to the sides of the trees. It is used to make tough, waterproof items such as rain boots.

Internet links

Go to **www.usborne-quicklinks.com** for links to the following Web sites:

Web site 1 Find out about natural and synthetic polymers.

Web site 2 Explore a virtual polymer "mall" for lots of great information.

Web site 3 An introduction to plastics and polymers.

Web site 4 More on polymers – an animated introduction.

Web site 5 Learn about super-strong Kevlar®, the bulletproof "wonder material".

Web site 6 An introduction to PVC (vinyl).

USING PLASTICS

Plastics are extremely versatile. They have been developed to the point where they are now used to make all sorts of different appliances, toys, tools and gadgets. Here are some examples of common plastics, along with examples of how they are used.

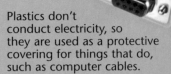

Plastics don't conduct electricity, so they are used as a protective covering for things that do, such as computer cables.

THE FIRST PLASTICS

The first plastics were made over 150 years ago. After early experiments, celluloid and then Bakelite were developed. Early in the twentieth century, Bakelite was used to make equipment such as radios and telephones.

Bakelite is heavy, so lighter plastics were developed to take its place.

This mobile phone has a lightweight case made from polypropene.

A 1930s telephone made from Bakelite

POLYTHENE

Polythene was first made in the 1930s. It can be made into thick, chunky shapes, or drawn out into very thin sheets.

Polythene is used to make many different things, from tough buckets to lightweight grocery bags.

Polythene is a good material for everyday products because it is easily molded and doesn't break if you drop it.

Polythene is waterproof so it is good for molding into bath toys such as these ducks.

These polythene ducks are safe for children. Some plastics, though, are never used for toys because they can give off poisonous chemicals if chewed.

POLYSTYRENE

Polystyrene is a plastic which sets firm. It can be made into lightweight foam which is a very good insulator. It is used for packaging food and fragile equipment.

Polystyrene packaging keeps food warm.

Polystyrene cup

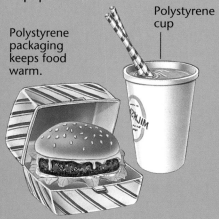

COMPOSITES

Many modern plastics can be combined to make even stronger materials called **composites**. These are used in spacecraft, aircraft, car components and sporting goods as they are stronger and lighter than more traditional materials.

Windsurfing boards are made of plastics reinforced with carbon or synthetic fibers.

Sails made of plastic fiber called Mylar® are extremely strong and light.

This remotely operated vehicle is used for underwater filming and gathering samples. It is made from plastics, which do not corrode.

Transparent, shatterproof PVC covering for video camera.

PLASTICS IN SPACE

Since space exploration began in the 1950s, lots of research has been done into finding new, lightweight, tough fabrics to protect astronauts. This has resulted in the invention of new plastics, such as those mentioned below.

Space suits contain eight or nine layers of plastic fabrics that can resist extremes of cold and heat.

Outer surface of the suit, made of super-strong plastic fiber called Kevlar®.

Inner suit of polyurethane-coated nylon mixed with polyester fiber.

Layers of a plastic fabric called Mylar® insulate against the cold.

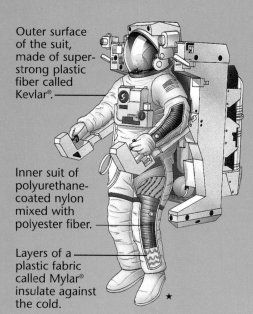

PLASTIC PROTECTION

Plastics can be both strong enough to resist impact and light enough to wear, making them ideal for protective headgear.

Football helmets are made of polycarbonate.

The steel face mask is coated with polyvinyl.

Helmets for race drivers are made of thermosetting plastic reinforced with Kevlar®. The gloves are made of a fire-resistant plastic called Nomex®.

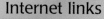

Internet links

Go to **www.usborne-quicklinks.com** for links to the following Web sites:

Web site 1 Take an online tour and learn about the life cycle of plastic products.

Web site 2 Find an online exhibition which explores the hidden world of materials, including plastics – and take an online quiz.

STRUCTURE OF AN ATOM

The elements of which mixtures and compounds are made are themselves built up of incredibly tiny particles called **atoms**. Atoms are so small that a sheet of paper, such as those that make up this book, is probably a million atoms thick.

SUBATOMIC PARTICLES

Atoms are made up of smaller particles called **subatomic particles**. In the middle of every atom is its **nucleus**. This contains two types of subatomic particles, called **protons** and **neutrons**.

A third type of subatomic particle, called **electrons**, whizz around the nucleus. They move in different levels, called **shells**. Each shell can have up to a certain number of electrons. When it is full, a new shell is started. The first shell holds two electrons; the second holds eight. Further shells may hold up to 18.

● **Protons** have a positive electrical charge. The number of protons in an atom's nucleus is called its **atomic number**. Each element has a different atomic number.

● **Neutrons** have no charge, so they are electrically neutral. The more protons and neutrons in an atom, the greater its mass (the amount of matter it contains). The number of protons and neutrons in an element is called its **mass number**. Electrons are not counted when calculating the mass number, as they add so little to an atom's mass.

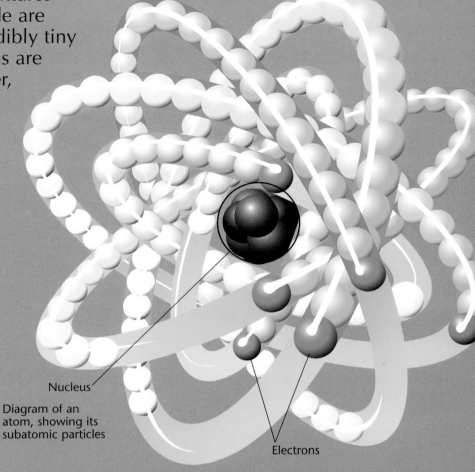

Nucleus

Diagram of an atom, showing its subatomic particles

Electrons

Atoms of one element usually exist in different forms, with different numbers of neutrons. These forms are called **isotopes**. Isotopes of an element have the same atomic number, but different mass numbers. This gives them different physical properties.

Electrons have a negative electrical charge. They are attracted to the protons' positive charge. This attraction is what holds atoms together. Atoms have an equal number of protons and electrons. This makes them electrically neutral.

● Electrons in first shell

● Electrons in second shell

PICTURING ATOMS

Although atoms are often represented by diagrams like the one above, scientists now believe that the electrons are held in cloud-like regions around the nucleus, as in the **electron cloud model**, below.

Electrons can be anywhere within their cloud, at any time. Sometimes they even move outside it.

FACTS AND LISTS

ORGANIC COMPOUNDS

Any compound which contains carbon atoms is described as **organic**. There are over two million different organic compounds, more than any other kind.

Here, you will find a summary of some common organic compounds, grouped in series. Within a series, the compounds are **homologous**, that is, they have similar chemical properties but their physical properties change as the molecules get larger. A representative group of members is shown for each series.

NAMING ORGANIC COMPOUNDS

The number of carbon atoms in a molecule of any organic compound is shown by the prefix at the beginning of its name. The first ten prefixes are given below.

Carbon atoms	Prefix	Carbon atoms	Prefix
One	meth-	Six	hex-
Two	eth-	Seven	hept-
Three	prop-	Eight	oct-
Four	but-	Nine	non-
Five	pent-	Ten	dec-

ALKANES

Alkanes burn in air to form carbon dioxide and water, and react with halogens. Other than that, they are unreactive. All except methane are obtained from crude oil.

Name	Molecular formula	Structural formula
Methane	CH_4	CH_4
Ethane	C_2H_6	CH_3CH_3
Propane	C_3H_8	$CH_3CH_2CH_3$
Butane	C_4H_{10}	$CH_3(CH_2)_2CH_3$
Pentane	C_5H_{12}	$CH_3(CH_2)_3CH_3$
Hexane	C_6H_{14}	$CH_3(CH_2)_4CH_3$
Heptane	C_7H_{16}	$CH_3(CH_2)_5CH_3$
Octane	C_8H_{18}	$CH_3(CH_2)_6CH_3$

ALKENES

Alkene molecules contain one or more double bonds between carbon atoms. Because of this, they are more reactive than alkanes – they undergo addition reactions, and some form polymers. Alkenes are used to make many products, including plastics.

Name	Molecular formula	Structural formula
Ethene	C_2H_4	$CH_2=CH_2$
Propene	C_3H_6	$CH_3CH=CH_2$
1-Butene	C_4H_8	$CH_3CH_2CH=CH_2$
1-Pentene	C_5H_{10}	$CH_3CH_2CH_2CH=CH_2$
Hexene	C_6H_{12}	$CH_3CH_2CH_2CH_2CH=CH_2$
Heptene	C_7H_{14}	$CH_3CH_2CH_2CH_2CH_2CH=CH_2$

ALKYNES

Alkynes, also known as acetylenes, have triple bonds between their carbon atoms (indicated with the symbol $\equiv$). They burn with a sooty flame in air and a very hot flame in pure oxygen. Alkynes are used to make plastics and solvents.

Name	Molecular formula	Structural formula
Ethyne	C_2H_2	$CH \equiv CH$
Propyne	C_3H_4	$CH_3C \equiv CH$
But-2-yne	C_4H_6	$CH_3C \equiv CCH_3$
Pentyne	C_5H_8	$CH_3CH_2CH_2C \equiv CH$

ALCOHOLS

Alcohols are organic compounds that contain carbon, oxygen and hydrogen. Moving down the series, the members gradually change from liquids to solids as their molecules get longer. Their boiling points also increase. Ethanol is the most commonly used alcohol.

Name	Molecular formula	Structural formula
Methanol	CH_4O	CH_3OH
Ethanol	C_2H_6O	$CH_3CH_2 OH$
1-Propanol	C_3H_8O	$CH_3CH_2CH_2OH$
1-Butanol	$C_4H_{10}O$	$CH_3CH_2CH_2CH_2OH$

USES OF POLYMERS

Here are some well-known polymers, with information on how they are commonly used.
It is worth remembering that while all plastics are polymers, not all polymers are plastics.
Look under "Properties" to see which is which.

Name	Properties	Used to make
Acrylic	Water-resistant polymer	Paints and varnishes
Bakelite	The first widely manufactured plastic. Heavier than modern plastics	Early telephones and other household objects
Celluloid (cellulose nitrate)	Highly flammable, transparent plastic	Movie film, billiard balls
Cellulose	Natural fibrous polymer found in wood and cotton	Used to make early synthetic polymers such as celluloid
High density polyethylene	Tough plastic	Milk and juice bottles
Kevlar®	Super-strong plastic fiber	Outer skin of space suits, sports equipment
Latex (polyisoprene)	Natural polymer, produced by rubber trees	Medical and office supplies, tires, protective clothing (e.g. gloves)
Lycra®	Stretchable synthetic fiber	Combined with other fibers to make stretchable clothing
Melamine	Rigid, heat-retardant thermoplastic	Mugs, plates and kitchen work surfaces
Mylar®	Strong, light, plastic fiber	Spacesuits, sails, balloons
Neoprene® (polychloroprene)	Tough, hardwearing plastic	Vehicle fanbelts, wetsuits
Nomex®	Flame-retardant polymer	Protective clothing
Nylon	Synthetic silk substitute	Parachutes, clothing
Polybutadiene	Hard synthetic rubber	Car parts, hoses, belts
Polycarbonate	A clear plastic	Eyeglass lenses, shatterproof windows
Polyethylene terephthalate (PET)	Clear, tough plastic, with good gas and moisture barrier properties	Carbonated drink bottles, jars
Polytetrafluoroethene (PTFE): commonly known as Teflon®	Unreactive, extremely slippery polymer	Non-stick cookware, carpet and fabric protection, Gore-tex® products
Polymethyl methacrylate (perspex)	Clear plastic, used as safer substitute for glass	Windows, eyeglasses
Polypropene	Lightweight plastic	Food containers
Polystyrene	Easily molded, firm-setting plastic which can be made into a compressable, plastic foam	Lightweight packing material, disposable cups
Polythene	Versatile, stretchable plastic	Grocery bags, cups, toothbrushes etc.
PVC (polyvinylchloride)	Easy to clean, waterproof, corrosion-resistant plastic	Clothing and fabrics, car interiors, bubble wrap
Rayon (cellulose xanthate)	Synthetic fibrous polymer	Clothing
Silicone	Elastic synthetic polymer	Heat-retardant tiles, hair treatments
Silk	Natural polymer made by silkworms	Soft fabrics

Polymer Web sites

Go to **www.usborne-quicklinks.com** for links to Web sites about polymers, including Kevlar®, Teflon®, Nomex® and Lycra®. You will also find links to Web sites which offer a fascinating introduction to a number of plastics, such as polystyrene.

P.18 Bonding answers

Element	Atomic number	Electron configuration
Magnesium	12	2, 8, 2
Argon	18	2, 8, 8
Nitrogen	7	2, 5
Potassium	19	2, 8, 8, 1
Silicon	14	2, 8, 4

TEST YOURSELF

1. Which of the following is not a mixture?
A. air
B. sea water
C. carbon dioxide   *(Page 8)*

2. Dyes can be separated by:
A. distillation
B. filtration
C. chromatography   *(Pages 10-11)*

3. An insoluble solid can be separated from a liquid by:
A. evaporation
B. filtration
C. chromatography   *(Page 10)*

4. A soluble solid can be separated from a liquid by:
A. evaporation
B. filtration
C. chromatography   *(Page 11)*

5. The most abundant gas in the atmosphere is:
A. carbon dioxide
B. nitrogen
C. oxygen   *(Page 12)*

6. Ozone is a form of:
A. nitrogen
B. oxygen
C. argon   *(Page 15)*

7. The build-up of which gas causes the greenhouse effect?
A. carbon dioxide
B. oxygen
C. argon   *(Page 15)*

8. What is formed when atoms of different elements combine?
A. a new element
B. a compound
C. a mixture   *(Page 16)*

9. Which of the following is not an example of a compound?
A. glass
B. salt
C. carbon   *(Page 17)*

10. The forces holding atoms together are known as bonds. Which of these is not a type of bonding?
A. covalent
B. valency
C. ionic   *(Pages 19-21)*

11. The second electron shell can hold up to:
A. two electrons
B. eighteen electrons
C. eight electrons   *(Page 18)*

12. Many covalent substances:
A. dissolve in water
B. conduct electricity
C. are liquids or gases at room temperature   *(Page 19)*

13. An atom that has lost electrons is:
A. an anion
B. a cation
C. an ionic lattice   *(Page 20)*

14. Which statement is false?
A. the chemical name for water is hydrogen oxide
B. ice is more dense than water
C. water can exist in three states: gas, liquid and solid   *(Page 22)*

15. Reactions in which heat is given out to the surroundings are:
A. exothermic
B. endothermic
C. thermal   *(Page 26)*

16. A catalyst:
A. changes the rate of a reaction and is used up in the reaction
B. changes the rate of a reaction and is not used up in the reaction
C. is a substance that stops a reaction from taking place *(Page 29)*

17. Combustion reactions need:
A. carbon monoxide
B. carbon dioxide
C. oxygen   *(Page 30)*

18. During reduction, a substance:
A. loses oxygen
B. loses hydrogen
C. loses electrons   *(Page 31)*

19. Which metal is extracted from bauxite by electrolysis?
A. aluminum
B. copper
C. iron   *(Page 33)*

20. Which of these is not a base?
A. toothpaste
B. tomato juice
C. wasp sting   *(Pages 34-35)*

21. Which statement is incorrect? Acids are
A. compounds that contain hydrogen
B. corrosive
C. caustic   *(Pages 34-35)*

22. The pH value of any acidic substance is:
A. less than 7
B. 7
C. more than 7   *(Page 36)*

23. Salts contain:
A. metals only
B. metals and non-metals
C. non-metals only   *(Page 38)*

24. All organic compounds contain:
A. silicon
B. oxygen
C. carbon   *(Page 42)*

25. Saturated organic compounds are held together by:
A. single bonds
B. double bonds
C. triple bonds   *(Page 43)*

26. The most important product of the fermentation reaction is an:
A. alkane
B. alkene
C. alcohol   *(Page 44)*

27. Margarine is made by adding hydrogen to:
A. alkane molecules
B. alkene molecules
C. ester molecules   *(Page 47)*

28. The chemical process in which large molecules from crude oil are split into smaller molecules is:
A. fractional distillation
B. hydrogenation
C. cracking   *(Pages 47, 49)*

29. What type of organic compounds condense at 180°C?
A. residue compounds
B. gasoline compounds
C. kerosene compounds   *(Page 49)*

30. Which of these statements about thermoplastics is true?
A. they are easily recycled
B. they can only be molded once
C. they are heat resistant   *(Page 51)*

A-Z OF SCIENTIFIC TERMS

Acid A compound that contains hydrogen and dissolves in water to produce hydrogen ions.

acid rain Rain that has increased in acidity after absorbing polluting gases such as sulfur dioxide and nitrogen dioxide.

activation energy The minimum amount of energy needed to start off a chemical reaction.

addition reaction A chemical reaction in which the double or triple bonds of an unsaturated compound open up and new bonds are formed with different atoms.

alcohols A homologous series of organic compounds with the general formula $C_nH_{2n+1}OH$. For example, ethanol is C_2H_5OH.

alkali A base that can dissolve in water, making an alkaline solution.

alkanes A homologous series of saturated hydrocarbons with the general formula C_nH_{2n+2}. For example, ethane is C_2H_6. They burn easily and many are used as fuels.

alkenes A homologous series of unsaturated hydrocarbons with the general formula C_nH_{2n}. For example, ethene is C_2H_4. They are used in industry to make plastics such as polythene.

alkynes A homologous series of unsaturated hydrocarbons with the general formula C_nH_{2n-2}. For example, ethyne is C_2H_2. They are used to make plastics and solvents.

allotropes Different forms in which certain elements, such as carbon, can exist. In each allotrope the (same) atoms are bonded together in a different way.

anhydrous The term describing the dry solid that results from dehydration.

anion A negatively charged ion.

anode In electrolysis, the electrode with the positive charge.

anodizing A method of coating a metal with a thin layer of its oxide using electrolysis, in order to prevent corrosion.

atomic number The number of protons in the nucleus of an atom.

atoms The tiny particles from which elements are made. Each atom has a positively charged nucleus, consisting of protons and (except hydrogen) neutrons. This is usually balanced by enough negatively charged electrons to make the atom electrically neutral. See also *ion; isotopes*.

Avogadro number The number of atoms or molecules found in one mole of a substance, which is 6.023×10^{23}.

Base A substance that can accept the hydrogen ions of an acid and is the chemical opposite of an acid. A base that dissolves in water is an alkali.

buckminsterfullerene A very strong allotrope of carbon with spherical molecules (often called buckyballs) containing 60 atoms.

Carbon cycle The process by which carbon (as carbon dioxide) enters the food chain from the atmosphere through photosynthesis and returns to the atmosphere through respiration and decay. See also *internal respiration*.

carboxylic acids Organic acids that contain a carboxyl group (–COOH).

catalyst A substance that changes the rate of a chemical reaction but is itself left unchanged.

catalytic converter A device attached to cars which uses metal catalysts, for example platinum and rhodium, to remove toxic gases from the exhaust fumes.

cathode In electrolysis, the electrode with the negative charge.

cation A positively charged ion.

centrifuging Spinning a suspension around very quickly to separate out the suspended solid particles from the liquid.

chemical formula A combination of chemical symbols, showing the atoms of which a substance is made and their proportions.

chemical reaction An interaction between substances in which their atoms are rearranged to form new substances. See also *product; reactants*.

chemical symbol A shorthand way of representing a specific element in formulae and equations.

chromatogram A pattern of colored bands made on filter paper or in a tube by substances separated by chromatography.

chromatography Separating the substances in a mixture by the rate they move through or along a medium, such as filter paper.

cleavage plane The boundary between the regular lines of particles in a crystal, along which the crystal can be split.

combination reaction See *synthesis reaction*.

combining power See *valency*.

combustion (or **burning**) An oxidation reaction, where a substance combines with oxygen to form an oxide, releasing energy as heat.

composites Synthetic materials, especially plastics, made up of different substances combined to improve their properties.

corrosion The process by which the surface of a metal reacts with oxygen to form the oxide of the metal. See also *rust*.

covalent bond A bond formed between two atoms, in which one or more electrons from one atom are attracted to the other's nucleus, and vice versa. As a result, the electrons are shared by both atoms.

cracking A method of changing organic compounds with large molecules into more useful compounds with smaller molecules.

crude oil A dark, thick mixture of hydrocarbons, from which many fuels and other chemicals are obtained by fractional distillation.

Decantation A method of separating solid, insoluble particles from a liquid by leaving the particles to settle and pouring off the liquid.

decomposition reaction A reaction in which a single compound breaks down into the substances that make it up. If heat is needed for the reaction, it is called a **thermal decomposition reaction**.

dehydrating agent A substance which removes water that is chemically combined in another (hydrated) substance.

dehydration The process by which water is removed from a hydrated solid, by heating or by the use of a dehydrating agent.

deionization A method of purifying water by filtering it through an ion exchange resin. The ions causing the impurity are removed by exchanging them for ions from the resin, which combine to form new water molecules.

diamond An allotrope of carbon with each atom linked to four others in a tight formation, forming extremely hard, four-sided crystals.

displacement reaction A chemical reaction in which one of the elements in a compound is replaced by a more reactive element.

distillation A method of obtaining a pure liquid from a solution by collecting the liquid as it evaporates, then allowing it to condense.

double bond A covalent bond in which a pair of atoms shares two pairs of electrons.

Electrode In electrolysis, a conductor through which the current enters or leaves the electrolyte.

electrolysis A method of splitting the elements in a compound by passing an electric current through it when it is molten or in a solution.

electrolyte The molten or dissolved substance that conducts an electric current during electrolysis.

electron A negatively charged particle that moves around the nucleus of an atom.

electron configuration The number of electrons that exist in each of the shells around the nuclei of the atoms of a particular element.

electron shell A region (level) around an atom's nucleus in which a certain number of electrons can exist.

electroplating A method of covering an object with a thin layer of metal by electrolysis.

electrorefining A method of purifying metals using electrolysis.

element A substance made up of atoms of the same type, all with the same atomic number. It cannot be broken down by a chemical reaction to form simpler substances. See also *isotopes*.

emulsifier A substance that helps two immiscible liquids, such as oil and water, to mix, by breaking up one of the liquids into tiny drops. The result is an emulsion.

emulsion A mixture of tiny particles of one liquid dispersed in another.

endothermic reaction A chemical reaction that takes in heat energy.

enzyme A catalyst that speeds up a chemical reaction in living things.

equation A way of showing chemical reactions using chemical formulae. The reactants are written to the left of an arrow which points to the products on the right.

esters A homologous series produced by carboxylic acids reacting with alcohols. They give fruit and flowers their flavors and fragrances.

evaporation 1. The process by which the surface molecules of a liquid escape into the air, becoming a vapor. 2. A method of separating a solute from a solvent by heating the solution until the solvent turns to vapor.

exothermic reaction A chemical reaction that gives off heat energy.

Fatty acids Carboxylic acids found in natural fats and oils.

fermentation A chemical reaction in which sugar is broken down by enzymes to produce ethanol and carbon dioxide.

filtration A method of separating solid, insoluble particles from a liquid by trapping them in a material (the **filter**) that lets only the liquid (the **filtrate**) pass through.

fossil fuel A fuel such as coal, oil or natural gas, that is formed from the fossilized remains of plants or animals.

fractional distillation A process by which substances are separated from a mixture by boiling in a tower called a **fractionating column**. The substances (called **fractions**) have different boiling points, and so separate off at different levels.

Global warming A rise in average temperatures around the world which scientists believe to be caused by the greenhouse effect.

graphite A soft, flaky allotrope of carbon in which each atom is linked to three others in a layered formation.

greenhouse effect The trapping of heat by carbon dioxide in the Earth's atmosphere.

Halite See *rock salt*.

hard water Water which contains a lot of dissolved minerals from rocks it has flowed over. **Temporary hard water** contains minerals that can be removed by boiling. **Permanent hard water** contains minerals that cannot.

homologous series A group of organic compounds with the same chemical properties. Going up through the group, each new compound has larger molecules, though. This means that their physical states change.

hydrated A term describing a substance which has undergone hydration.

hydration The process by which water combines chemically with another substance.

hydrocarbon An organic compound that contains only hydrogen and carbon.

hydrogenation An addition reaction in which unsaturated molecules are saturated by adding hydrogen atoms.

hydroxyl group (–OH) An oxygen atom linked to a hydrogen atom by a covalent bond.

Immiscible The term that describes two or more liquids that do not mix together easily. See also *emulsifier*.

indicator A substance that changes color in the presence of an acid or alkali and is used to distinguish between them.

inhibitor A catalyst that slows down the rate of a chemical reaction.

internal respiration The process by which animals and plants use oxygen to break down their food, producing energy and releasing carbon dioxide.

ion An atom that has become electrically charged by gaining or losing one or more electrons. See also *anion*; *cation*.

ion exchange A method used to soften hard water by exchanging its dissolved calcium and magnesium ions for sodium ions.

ionic bond A strong bond caused by the attraction between ions of opposite charge.

ionic compound A compound consisting of bonded ions.

ionic lattice The structure made by the ions of an ionic compound. They are all held together in one regular arrangement by their ionic bonds, rather than as individual molecules.

isotopes Different forms of the same element. The atoms of each isotope have the same number of protons, but a different number of neutrons, in their nuclei. So isotopes of an element have the same atomic number, but different mass numbers.

Liquid crystals Crystals that become cloudy upon heating. They are used to make patterns of light and dark in **liquid crystal displays** (**LCDs**), for example in digital watches.

litmus A substance extracted from lichens that is used as an indicator.

Mass number The total number of protons and neutrons in the nucleus of an atom. The mass number of two atoms of the same element may be different, because they may be different isotopes.

metallic bonding The way the atoms of metal elements bond – clinging together in a regular lattice of metal cations with free electrons flowing between them.

minerals The naturally occurring single elements and compounds of which rocks are made.

miscible The term that describes two or more liquids that mix easily.

mole The SI unit of the amount of a substance, i.e. the number of particles (atoms or molecules). See also *Avogadro number*.

molecular lattice A regular structure of molecules held together by weak forces, as in iodine, for example. The molecules break apart quite easily.

molecule The smallest particle of an element or compound that exists on its own and keeps its properties.

monomers Small molecules that are joined together to make a polymer.

Neutralization reaction A reaction where one reactant fully or partly cancels out the properties of another, for example, when an acid and a base react to form a salt and water.

neutron A subatomic particle with no electrical charge. Neutrons form part of the nuclei of every atom (except those of hydrogen).

nitrogen cycle The natural process in which nitrogen is converted into nitrates in the soil, used by plants, and returned again to the air.

noble gases The six highly unreactive elements (all gases) present in the atmosphere which together form group VIII of the periodic table. They are helium, neon, argon, krypton, xenon and radon.

nucleus The core section of an atom that contains protons and (except hydrogen) neutrons.

Organic compound A compound that contains the element carbon.
oxidation A chemical reaction in which a substance combines with oxygen, or loses hydrogen or electrons.

oxide A compound of oxygen and another element.

oxidizing agent A substance that provides oxygen or receives electrons or hydrogen, during oxidation.

ozone (O_3) A poisonous allotrope of oxygen. It forms the protective ozone layer in the upper atmosphere, which absorbs harmful ultraviolet radiation from the Sun.

Periodic table A systematic arrangement of the elements in order of increasing atomic number.
pH The strength of an acid or base expressed as a number on a scale from 0 (strongly acidic) to 14 (strongly alkaline).

photochemical reaction A chemical reaction that gives off or takes in light energy.

physical states See *states of matter.*

piezoelectric effect The regular vibration produced by applying a voltage between the faces of a crystal such as quartz. It is used to measure time.

plastics Easily-molded synthetic polymers made from the organic compounds obtained from crude oil. See also *thermoplastics; thermosetting plastics.*

polymer A substance with long-chain molecules, made up of many small molecules called monomers. Substances such as cellulose and latex are examples of natural polymers, and many synthetic polymers are used in everyday life and in industry.

polymerization The process of joining monomers to make polymers.

precipitate An insoluble solid that separates from a solution during a chemical reaction.

product A new substance produced by a chemical reaction. See also *reactants.*

proton A positively charged subatomic particle. Protons form part of the nucleus of every atom.

Quarks Particles which are believed to make up protons and neutrons.

Reactants The substances which come together in a chemical reaction. See also *product.*

reactivity The tendency of a substance to react with other substances.

reactivity series A list of elements, usually metals, arranged in order of how easily they react with other substances.

redox reaction A chemical reaction in which both reduction and oxidation take place.

reducing agent A substance that takes oxygen from another substance during reduction, or loses electrons or hydrogen.

reduction A chemical reaction in which a substance loses oxygen, or gains hydrogen or electrons.

reversible reaction A reaction in which the products can, under the right conditions, react together to form the original reactants.

rock salt (or **halite**) The mineral form of common salt (sodium chloride).

rust Iron oxide that forms on the surface of iron, or an iron alloy, due to corrosion. It gradually flakes off, causing the iron to deteriorate.

Salt 1. A compound of a metal and non-metal, produced when one or more of the hydrogen ions in an acid are replaced by metal or ammonium ions. 2. The common name for sodium chloride (NaCl).

saturated compound An organic compound whose molecules contain only single covalent bonds.

saturated solution A solution in which no more solute will dissolve.

shell See *electron shell.*

single bond A covalent bond in which a pair of atoms shares one pair of electrons.

SI units An internationally agreed system of standard units used for scientific measurement.

smelting The process of extracting a metal, usually iron, from its ore by heating to high temperatures, and reducing the ore.

solution A mixture that consists of a substance (the **solute**) dissolved in a liquid.

solvent 1. A liquid that can dissolve other substances. 2. The liquid in which a substance is dissolved.

states of matter (or **physical states**) The different forms in which a substance can exist. The three basic states are solid, liquid and gas.

strong acid An acid in which most of the molecules separate to become hydrogen ions when in solution. For example, hydrochloric acid.

subatomic particles Particles smaller than an atom, especially those of which atoms are made: protons, electrons and neutrons.

substitution reaction A chemical reaction in which some of the single bonds in the molecules of a saturated compound break open, and their atoms are replaced by atoms of another element.

suspension A mixture of solid particles floating in a liquid or gas.

synthesis (or **combination**) **reaction** A reaction in which substances combine to make a single new substance.

synthetic fibers Fibers, such as nylon fibers, that are produced artificially by drawing out plastics into fine strands.

Thermal decomposition reaction See *decomposition reaction.*

thermoplastics Plastics which can be melted and used again.

thermosetting plastics Plastics which can be molded only once.

triple bond A covalent bond in which a pair of atoms shares three pairs of electrons.

Universal indicator An indicator made of a mixture of dyes that change color according to the pH scale.

unsaturated compound An organic compound whose molecules have at least one double or triple covalent bond.

Valency (or **combining power**) The number of electrons an atom must gain or lose to acquire a stable outer shell.

vulcanization The heating of rubber with sulfur, in order to strengthen it.

Water cycle The natural process by which water is recycled between the Earth, the atmosphere and living things.

water of crystallization Water that has loosely chemically bonded with another substance, making a hydrated form of the substance.

waxes A group of solid esters, many of which are produced by living things. They are usually glossy, easily molded and insoluble in water.

weak acid An acid that contains relatively few hydrogen ions when in solution, for example ethanoic acid.

INDEX

You will find the main explanations of terms in the index on the pages shown in bold type. It may be useful to look at the other pages for further information.

1,2-dibromoethane **43**

A

acid rain 14, **15**, 36, 58
acids 15, 28, **34**, 36-37, 38, 39, 44, 58
acrylic **51**, 56
action specific (catalysts) **29**
activation energy **26**, 29, 58
addition reactions **43**, 47, 58
aerosol **43**
air **12-15**
aircraft 53
alcohols **44**, 45, 55, 58
alkalis 28, 34, **35**, 36, 37, 38, 44, 58
alkanes 42, **46**, 47, 49, 55, 58
alkenes 42, 46, **47**, 50, 55, 58
alkynes **55**
allotropes 21, 58
alum **41**
aluminum **33**, 41
    oxide **33**
amethyst **40**
amine 51
ammonia **14**
ammonium
    hydroxide **35**
    sulfate **37**
anhydrous **41**, 58
aniline **42**
anions **20**, 32, 58
anodes **32**, 33, 58
anodizing **33**, 58
apatite **40**
argon **13**, 18
ascorbic acid **34**
astronauts **53**
atmosphere **12**, 15
atom 18-21, 26, **54**
atomic
    number 18, **54**, 58
Avogadro number **27**, 58

B

backward reaction **28**
bacteria 14, 24, 25
Bakelite **52**, 56
base 34, **35**, 36, 38, 39, 58
bauxite **33**
bicarbonate of soda 35, 37
blood 8, **11**

boiling point 19, 20, 22
bonding (atoms) **18-21**, 26, 29, 41, 42-43, 46-47, 55
brass 32
breathing **12-13**
brine **39**
bromine **43**
buckminsterfullerene **21**, 58
bulb, light 13
burning (See *combustion*)
    fuels 13, 14
butane **46**, 55

C

cadmium sufide 38
calcite **40**
calcium 23, 38
    carbonate 17, **23**, 26, 28, 36, 38
    hydrogencarbonate **23**
    hydroxide **36**
    oxide **28**
    sulfate **38**
car 53
carbon 19, 21, 31, **42-53**, 55
    cycle, **58**
    dioxide 12, **13**, 15, 16, 19, 23, 28, 30, 31, 34, 35, 50
    monoxide **14**, 29
carbonates 26, 34, **38**
carbonic acid **13**, 23, 29, 38
carboxylic acids **44**, 45, 51, 58
catalysts **29**, 58
catalytic converters **29**, 58
cathodes **32**, 33, 58
cations **20**, 32, 58
caustic **35**
    soda **35**, 39
celluloid 52, 56
cellulose 35, **56**
centrifuging **11**, 58
CFCs (See *chlorofluorocarbons*)
chalk 36, **38**
chemical
    equations **27**, 58
    formulae **16**, 58
    reactions **26-29**, 30-31, 55, 58
    symbols **58**
chlorides 16, **38**
chlorine 16, 17, 30, 39, 43, 46, 50
chloroethene **50**
chlorofluorocarbons (CFCs) 43, **46**
cholesterol 47
chromatogram **10**, 58
chromatography **10**, 58
chromium **32**
citric acid 17, **34**, 50
cleavage plane **40**
clouds **24**
coal **14**
combination reactions **28**, 58
combining power **21**, 58
combustion 12, 28, **30**, 58

composites **53**, 58
compounds 8, **16-17**, 18-25
conservation of mass **27**
copper 28, 30, 33
    oxide 31, 39
    copper (II) chloride **32**
    sulfate 28, 33, **39**, 41
corrosion 15, 33, 34, **58**
cosmetics **17**
covalent bonding **19**, 42, 46, 47, 58
cracking (molecules) **49**, 58
crude oil 46, **48-49**, 50, 55, 58
cryolite 33
crystals 37, 38, 39, **40-41**

D

decane **49**
decantation **10**, 58
decomposition reactions **28**, 58
dehydrating agent **37**, 41, 58
dehydration **41**, 58
deionization **25**, 58
detergents 25, 37, **44**, 45
diamond **21**, 40, 58
dichlorodifluoromethane 43, **46**
diesel oil **49**
digestion 29
digestive enzymes **29**
displacement reactions **28**, 58
distillation **11**, 25, 58
dodecanoic acid 44
double bonds **19**, 42, 43, 47, 55, 58
dyes 36, 37, **42**

E

electrodes **32**, 59
electrolysis **32-33**, 59
electrolyte **32**, 33, 59
electron 18, 20, 21, 25, 30, 31, 42, **54**, 59
    cloud model **54**
    configuration **18**, 59
    shells **18**, 21, 42, **54**, 59
electroplating **32**, 59
electrorefining **33**, 59
elements **8**, 59
emerald **40**
emulsifiers **9**, 59
emulsions **9**, 59
endothermic reactions **26**, 28, 59
enzymes **29**, 44, 59
equations **27**, 59
esters **45**, 59
ethane **42**, 47, 55
ethanoic acid 34, 35, **44**
ethanol 44, **55**
ethene 42, 43, 44, **47**, 49, 50, 55
evaporation **11**, 59
exhaust fumes 29
exothermic reactions **26**, 27, 28, 29, 59

F

fats **45**
fatty acids **44**, 59
fermentation **44**, 59
fertilizer 14, 25, 37, **39**
filters **10**, 59 (filtration)
filtrates **10**, 59 (filtration)
filtration **10**, 39, 59
fireworks 30
fluorine 18, 21, 43, 46
formic acid **34**
formulae, chemical **16**, 58
forward reaction **28**
fossil fuels 14, **48**, 59
fraction (oil) **49**, 59 (fractional distillation)
fractional distillation 12, 48, **49**, 59
fractionating column **49**, 59 (fractional distillation)
freezing point of water **22**
fuel 14, 30, 46, 48, 49

G

gas 8, 29
gasoline 46, 48, 49
giant molecules **19**
gills 12
global warming 13, **15**, 59
glucose **30**, **31**
glycerol **45**
graphite **21**, 33, 59
greenhouse effect 13, **15**, 59
gypsum 23

H

halite **39**, 41, 59
hard water **23**, 38, 44, 59
heat 26, 28
helium **13**
homologous series **42**, 44, 46, 47, 55, 59
humic acid **36**
hydrated **41**, 59
hydration 39, **41**, 59
hydrocarbons 29, **42**, 46, 47, 48, 59
hydrochloric acid **34**, 38, 39
hydrogen 18, 19, 22, 23, 30, 31, 33, 42, 43, 44, 47, 48
  ions 25, 33, **34**, 35, 36, 38
  oxide 16, **22**
hydrogenation **47**, 59
hydroxide ions **35**
hydroxyl group **44**, 59

I

ice **22**
immiscible **9**, 59
indicators **36**, 37, 59

inhibitors (catalyst) **29**, 59
insolubility **8**, 38
insulator 53
internal respiration **30**, 31, 59
iodine **20**
ion exchange **23**, 25, 59
ionic
  bonding **20**, 59
  compounds **20**, 23, 38, 59
  lattices **20**, 59
ions **20**, 21, 23, 25, 32, 33, 34, 35, 36, 38, 44, 59
iron 16, 27, 28, 30, 31, 40
  ore **31**
  oxide **31**
  pyrites **40**
  sulfide **16**, 27
isotopes 54, **59**

J

jet 46

K

kerosene **46**, 49
Kevlar **47**, 56
krypton **13**

L

latex **51**, 56
lattices **20**
lauric acid 44
LCDs (See *liquid crystal displays*)
lead 14, 25
lichens 36
light 28
lightning 14
limestone 23, 26, 28, 29, 36, 38
liquid crystals **40**
liquid crystal displays (LCDs) **40**
liquids 8, 9, 29
litmus **36**, 38, 59

M

magnesium 18, 23, 28, 30
  chloride **30**
  hydroxide 35
  oxide 28, 35
malachite 38
margarine 47
mass 27
  number **54**, 59
melamine **51**, 56
melting point 19, 20
mercury 25
metallic
  bonding **20**, 59
  lattice **20**
metals 32, 33, 38, 39
methane **42**, 43, 46, 55
methanoic acid 34, 44

mineral acids **37**
minerals 23, 40, 59
miscible **9**, 59
mixtures **8-11**, 12-15
moles 27, 59
molecular lattices **20**, 59
molecules 19, 20, 26, 29, 41, 49, 50, **59**
monomers **50**, 59
motorcycle 30

N

natural
  fibers 50, 51
  gas 46, 48
  polymers 50, **51**
neon **13**
neutralization reactions **28**, 35, 59
neutrons 60
nitrates **14**, 38, 39
nitric acid 14, 34, 38
nitrogen 12, **14**, 18
  cycle **14**, 60
  dioxide 15, 28
  monoxide 28
noble gases **13**, 60
Nomex **53**, 56
non-metals 38
nucleus 60
nylon 50, **51**, 53, 56

O

octane 49, 55
oil platform 48
oils 9, 45, 46, 48-49, 50
organic
  acids **34**, **44**
  chemistry **42-45**, 46-47, 49-51, **55**
  compounds **17**, **42**, 43, 44-50, **55**, 60
oxidation **30**, 31, 44, 60
oxides 16, 30, 33, 35, 39, 60
oxidizing agents **30**, 37, 60
oxygen **12**, 15, 19, 22, 23, 25, 28, 30, 31, 33, 44
ozone **15**, 60
  layer **15**, 60 (ozone)

P

paint 9, 38
periodic table **60**
perspex (polymethyl methacrylate) **56**
pesticides 25
pH numbers **36**, 60 (pH)
phosphates 25, 37, 39
phosphorus 21, 39
photochemical reactions **28**, 60
photosynthesis 28, **31**
physical states 27, 60
piezoelectric effect **41**, 60

pigments **17**
planes 46
plankton 48
plasma (in blood) 11
plaster of Paris **38**
plastics 47, **50-53**, **56**, 60
platelets 11
platinum 29
pollution 13, **14**, 15, **25**
polycarbonate 53, 56
polyester 44, **51**, 53
polymers **50**, **51**, **56**, 60
polymerization **50**, 60
polypropene 52, 56
polystyrene 50, 51, **53**, 56
polythene 47, 50, 51, **52**, 56
polyurethane 53
polyvinyl 53
polyvinylchloride (PVC) **43**, **50**, 53, 56
potash 39
potassium 18, 39, 41
precipitate **39**, 60
products **26**, 27, 28, 60
propan-1,2,3-triol 45
propane **42**, 46, 55
propene 47, 55
proteins 14, 51
protons 18, 20, 60
PVC (See *polyvinylchloride*)
pyrite **40**

Q

quarks 60
quartz **16**, 40, 41
    crystals **41**
quicklime **28**

R

radon **13**
rainwater 14, 15, 23, 29, 37
rayon 37, **56**
reactants **26**, 27, 28, 60
reactions, chemical **26-29**, 30-31, 55, 58
reactivity **29**, 32, 33, 60
    series **60**
recycling 51
red blood cells 11
redox reactions **30**, 60
reducing agents **31**, 60
reduction 30, **31**, 60
refinery gases **49**
reservoirs
    oil and gas **48**
    water 24
residue **10**
residue compounds 49
respiration, internal **30**, 31, 59
reversible reactions **28**, 60
rhodium 29
rock salt 39, 60

root (of a plant) 39
rubber 51
rusting **30**, 32, 60 (rust)

S

sails 53
salicylic acid 34
salt, common 16, **17**, 20, 38, **39**, 60
salts 34, 35, **38-39**, 40, 41, 44, 60
saturated
    compounds **43**, 46, 47, 60
    solutions **23**, 60
scum 23, 44
sea
    slugs 34
    water 8, **9**, 22, 24, 39
seed crystal **41**
sewage **24**
    works **24**
shell models of atoms **18**
shells, electron **18**, 20, 21, 42, **54**, 59
silicon 18
    dioxide 19
silk 56
single bonds **42**, 43, 46, 60
SI units **60**
slaked lime 36
smelting **31**, 60
smog **14**
smoke 8, 14
soap 23, 34, 35, **44**
    bubbles 44
sodium 16, 17, 18, 21
    aluminum silicate 23
    bicarbonate (See *bicarbonate of soda*)
    carbonate 23, 38, 39, 41 (washing soda)
    chloride 16, **17**, 20, 38, **39**
    ethanoate 35
    hydroxide **35**, 38, 39, 44
soil 36
solids 8, 29
solubility **8**, 38
solutes **8**, 60 (solution)
solutions 8, 9, 10, 11, 23, 39, 60
solvents **8**, 23, 60
space suits **53**
spacecraft 53
stability of atoms 18
starch 50
states of matter 27, **60**
steel 32
strong acids **34**, 60
strontium 30
subatomic particles **54**, 60
substitution reactions **43**, 60
sulfates 38
sulfur 16, 21, 27, 37, **39**, 40, 51
    dioxide **14**, 15
    trioxide 26
sulfuric acid 26, 33, 34, 37, 38,

39, 41
Sun 15
suspensions **8**, 11, 60
symbols, chemical 58
synthesis reactions **28**, 60
synthetic
    compounds **43**, 50-53 (synthetic polymers)
    fibers **37**, 47, 50, **51**, 53, 60

T

Teflon (polytetrafluoroethene) **56**
television 40
thermal decomposition reactions **28**, 60
thermoplastics **51**, 60
thermosetting plastics **51**, 53, 60
tin 32
tires 51
titanium oxide 37
triple bonds 42, **43**, 60
tufa tower **26**

U

ultraviolet (UV) rays 15
universal indicator 36, 60
unsaturated compounds **43**, 47, 60

V

valency **21**, 60
vermilion 38
vinegar 34, 35, 37, 44
vitamins 43
vulcanization 51, **60**

W

washing soda **23**, 38, 39, 41
water 10, 11, 16, 19, **22-25**, 26, 41, 44
    cycle **24**, 25, 60
    of crystallization **41**, 60
    purification **25**
    softening **23**
    vapor **22**, 24
waterworks **24**
waxes 60
weak acids **34**, 60
weather 15
white blood cells 11

X

xenon **13**

Z

zeolite 23
zinc 20

WEB SITES

ACKNOWLEDGEMENTS

ˉDr Keith Taber

PHOTO CREDITS
(t = top, m = middle, b = bottom, l = left, r = right)

Corbis: **6-7** W. Cody; **12-13** (main) Jonathan Blair; **14-15** (main) Ted Spiegal; **22-23** (b) Peter Johnson; **24-25** (b) Wolfgang Kaehler; **26-27** (main) Randy Faris; **35** (main) Robert Pickett; **37** (b) Jonathan Blair; **39** (tr) Science Pictures Limited; **45** (main) Michael Freeman; **48** (tr) Science Pictures Limited; **52** (b) Tecmap Corporation/Eric Curry, Eric Curry.
© **Digital Vision**: **cover**; **1**; **2-3**; **5**; **8-9**; **9** (ml); **14** (tl); **15** (t); **22** (tr); **25** (tr); **28**(b); **30** (br); **31** (r); **32** (t), (br); **35** (tl); **37** (l); **46** (b); **48-49**; **49** (tl); **51** (m); **52** (tr); **53** (br); **55**.
Science Photo Library: **cover** Tek Image; **8** (ml) Tek Image; **10-11** (main) Geoff Tompkinson; **11** (r) Tek Image; **21** (br) Ken Eward; **43** (br) Steve Horrell; **51** (br) Eye of Science.
Telegraph Colour Library 1 Tia Rygs; **30-31** (main).
Karrimor International Ltd 51 (ml); **Nokia Mobile Phones 52** (m)

ILLUSTRATORS

Simone Abel, Sophie Allington, Jane Andrews, Rex Archer, Paul Bambrick, Jeremy Banks, Andrew Beckett, Joyce Bee, Stephen Bennett, Roland Berry, Gary Bines, Isabel Bowring, Trevor Boyer, John Brettoner, Gerry Browne, Peter Bull, Hilary Burn, Andy Burton, Terry Callcut, Kuo Kang Chen, Stephen Conlin, Sydney Cornfield, Dan Courtney, Steve Cross, Gordon Davies, Peter Dennis, Richard Draper, Brin Edwards, John Francis, Mark Franklin, Peter Geissler, Nick Gibbard, William Giles, Mick Gillah, David Goldston, Peter Goodwin, Jeremy Gower, Teri Gower, Terry Hadler, Alan Harris, Nick Hawken, Nicholas Hewetson, Christine Howes, John Hutchinson, Ian Jackson, Hans Jessen, Karen Johnson, Richard Johnson, Elaine Keenan, Aziz Khan, Stephen Kirk, Richard Lewington, Brian Lewis, Jason Lewis, Steve Lings, Rachel Lockwood, Kevin Lyles, Chris Lyon, Kevin Maddison, Janos Marffy, Andy Martin, Josephine Martin, Rob McCaig, Joseph McEwan, David McGrail, Malcolm McGregor, Dee McLean, Annabel Milne, Robert Morton, Paddy Mounter, Louise Nevet, Martin Newton, Louise Nixon, Steve Page, Justine Peek, Maurice Pledger, Mick Posen, Russell Punter, Barry Raynor, Mark Roberts, Michael Roffe, Michelle Ross, Simon Roulstone, Graham Round, Michael Saunders, John Scorey, John Shackell, Chris Shields, David Slinn, Graham Smith, Guy Smith, Peter Stebbing, Ian Stephen, Sue Stitt, Stuart Trotter, Robert Walster, Craig Warwick, Ross Watton, Phil Weare, Hans Wiborg-Jenssen, Sean Wilkinson, Gerald Wood, David Wright, Nigel Wright.

American editor: Carrie A. Seay